**INSIGHT** POCKET GUIDE

ISTANBUL

Discovery
CHANNEL

APA PUBLICATIONS
Part of the Langenscheidt Publishing Group

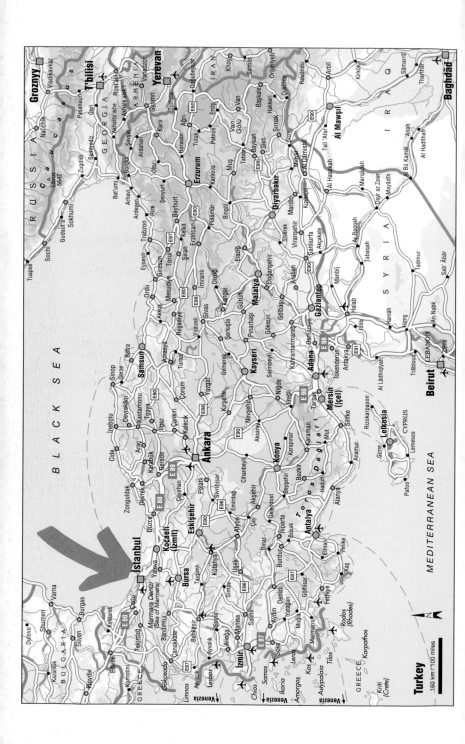

introduction

Welcome

This is one of 133 itinerary-based *Pocket Guides* produced by the editors of Insight Guides, whose books have set the standard for visual travel guides since 1970. With top-quality photography and authoritative recommendations, this guidebook aims to help visitors get the most out of Istanbul in a series of routes put together by Insight's correspondent in the city, Metin Demirsar.

Built on the banks of the Bosphorus, a strategic waterway linking the Sea of Marmara and the Black Sea, Istanbul has been the capital of three major empires – the Roman, Byzantine and Ottoman – and is filled with the riches of its glorious past. But the city is much more than its churches, mosques and palaces; it is also a vibrant modern metropolis, balanced between East and West at the point where Europe and Asia meet.

The tours begin with four full-day itineraries linking the must-see attractions, such as the Blue Mosque, Aya Sofya, Topkapı Palace, a boat ride along the Bosphorus, and a tour of the New City across the Golden Horn. These are followed by five shorter itineraries, designed to suit a range of tastes, from haggling for bargains in the Covered Bazaar to touring the sacred district of Eyüp along the Golden Horn. All the itineraries include detailed directions on getting around and stops for rest and refreshment.

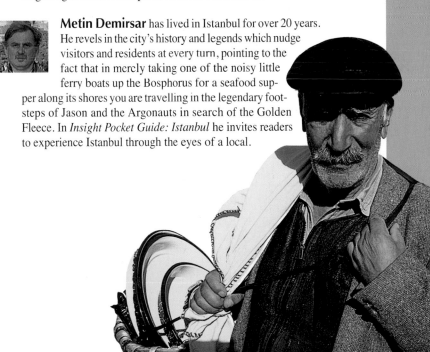

Metin Demirsar has lived in Istanbul for over 20 years. He revels in the city's history and legends which nudge visitors and residents at every turn, pointing to the fact that in merely taking one of the noisy little ferry boats up the Bosphorus for a seafood supper along its shores you are travelling in the legendary footsteps of Jason and the Argonauts in search of the Golden Fleece. In *Insight Pocket Guide: Istanbul* he invites readers to experience Istanbul through the eyes of a local.

HISTORY AND CULTURE

From the Romans, Byzantines and Ottomans right through to Kemal Atatürk and the birth of modern Turkey – a concise account of Istanbul's pivotal role as one of the world's most important commercial centres **11–17**

ITINERARIES

Pages 2–3: the Egyptian Obelisk and minarets
Following pages: a pillow merchant in the Old City

History & Culture

Located both on historic trade routes linking Europe and Asia, and a strategic sea lane connecting the Black Sea to the Mediterranean, Istanbul has been one of the world's most important commercial centres for some 2,700 years. The setting for myriad religions, sects and schisms as well as pageantry, military conquests, bloody riots, destructive fires, epidemics, earthquakes and daring architectural experiments, its history is as fascinating as it is contradictory.

The city has been known by various names. The Vikings, whose navies once tried, but failed to breach its walls, called it Mickligarth, 'the Great Enclosure'. To the Slavs of central Europe it was Tsargrad, 'Caesar's City', and to the Romans 'New Rome', as it was modelled after their capital.

City of the Blind

The earliest written records of Istanbul say it was founded by Greek King Byzas of Megara in 666BC, though there were isolated settlements on the Bosphorus from a much earlier date. Byzas, according to legend, was led to the spot after consulting the Oracle of Delphi. In a cryptic pronouncement, the oracle told him to construct his new town 'across from the city of the blind', and when Byzas reached the Bosphorus, he discovered a small colony called Chalcedon on its Asian shores, today the middle-class suburb of Kadıköy. These early settlers, Byzas deduced, had been so blind they had overlooked the most obvious and advantageous setting for a city. This is the hill on the European shore where Topkapı Palace stands today, commanding a stunning view of the Bosphorus, the Golden Horn and the Sea of Marmara. Byzas built his town on this hill and named it Byzantium.

Persian Domination

In 512BC, the Persians occupied the town. King Darius built a bridge of boats at the narrowest point of the Bosphorus to transport his army in an unsuccessful bid to conquer eastern Europe. But this domination ended in 479BC when the city reverted to Greek rule under Pausanias of Sparta.

The city repulsed an invasion of Celtic tribes, known as the Galatians or Gauls, in 279BC, but agreed to pay tribute, and some of these blond, blue-eyed Celts settled in Byzantium. The harbour district, which lies directly across the old city on the Golden Horn, has since been known as Galata.

In 179BC, Rhodes, Pergamum and Bithynia joined forces to capture the city, and Byzantium

Left: mosaic of Byzantine Emperor Justinian I
Right: Barberini Ivory of Emperor Anastasios I Dikoros

was eventually absorbed into the Roman Empire. Three centuries later, however, it sided with rebels in a Roman civil war and in AD193 was sacked and stripped of its privileges in punishment by Emperor Septimius Severus. Severus later re-built and repopulated the city, naming it Augusta Antonina in honour of his son Antonius Caracalla.

Constantine the Great

Ultimately, Byzantium capitulated to the Roman Emperor Constantine the Great, and in 324, the great era of 'New Rome' and Constantinople was born. This was the beginning of the Byzantine period which was to last more than 11 centuries, and the city was soon to become the first Christian capital of the Empire, leaving the former pagan capital of old Rome to falter.

Officially inaugurated in 330, Constantine's city was, like its predecessor,

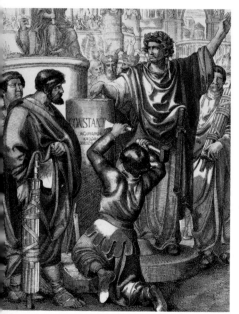

built on seven hills. In addition to paved roads, splendid palaces, fountains, gigantic cisterns, churches and public baths, some of which still stand today, the Emperor adorned it with monuments taken from the four corners of the Roman Empire, including the Egyptian Obelisk which stands in the Hippodrome in front of the Blue Mosque. Paganism – though not banned outright – was slowly phased out, its statues given new names and associated over time with the attributes of Christ and the emperors alike.

Gradually, Roman Asia Minor was assimilated into the Greco-Anatolian world, and by the time Rome fell in 476, the shift of power was nearly complete. The Greek language of Anatolia eventually replaced Latin, and the remaining part of the Roman state came to be known as the Byzantine Empire.

Constantine's successor, Valens (364–378), built giant aqueducts to transport water to the city from lakes north of Constantinople. Emperor Theodosius II (408–450) extended the city's land walls to their present boundaries, thus making the city almost impregnable. Emperor Anastasius (491–518) built peripheral walls, stretching from the Black Sea to Çatalca, to bolster the city's outer defences, following some dangerous raids by Bulgarian and Slavic tribes.

Constantinople also became the cultural centre of the empire. In addition to many schools of religion and lay education, a sumptuous tradition of iconography and court artisanship soon produced goods that were the envy of the world, and in particular the purple silks which were the preserve of the hierarchy. A population so well versed in theology, however, and exposed to such gaudy displays of church and palace, could not help but query such excess, a factor contributing to the iconoclastic movement, its ongoing dis-

Above: Constantine names his new city
Right: mosaic of Christ in Aya Sofya

putes over the human versus divine nature of Christ, and the morality of pictorial representation in religious art. Iconoclasm was to become state policy briefly in the 8th century, when Emperor Leo III smashed the magnificent mosaic of Christ over the entrance to the Palace, provoking a riot. But the enduring appeal of religious pictorial art triumphed during the Church Council of Nicaea in 787, restoring the adoration of icons.

The Nika Revolt

Sectarian alliances in Constantinople often fell behind the various 'colours'of chariot teams, not unlike soccer hooliganism today. The Nika Revolt of 532 started during a chariot race at the Hippodrome and led to the worst blood-bath the city has ever seen, burning much (including Aya Sofya) to the ground and killing 30,000 people. Emperor Justinian used an iron-fist rule to suppress the riot, but was provided with an excuse to rebuild the city as well as codify Roman law in keeping with Christian principles.

Over the next 900 years, Constantinople grew to become the biggest city in Europe and the Near East, a shimmering vision of wealth and splendour when Paris and London were but squalid towns. Despite many attacks on the stout city walls, notably by Arab armies in 668 and 718, the city kept covetous invaders in check until the late 11th century, when nomadic Central Asian warriors, the Turks, thundered across the Anatolian hinterland in a campaign of conquest under the banner of Islam.

In 1071, a Turkish army under Seljuk Sultan Alp Arslan routed the vastly superior numbers of the Byzantine army and captured Emperor Romanus IV Diogenes at Malazgirt (Manzikert) in eastern Anatolia. For the first time, the Byzantine Empire was threatened by foreigners.

Initially the Crusades, sponsored by the Papacy ostensibly to unify Catholic and Orthodox Christians, held back waves of Turkish horsemen. But in 1204 the Latins turned their rapacious eyes on Constantinople, sacking the city and plundering its wealth. They killed tens of thousands of Orthodox Christians, destroyed many magnificent buildings and carried off priceless relics to Venice, including the bronze horses at St Mark's Cathedral. A Latin state

was forced on Constantinople and the Byzantine Emperors fled to nearby Nicaea, modern day Iznik. Although the Byzantines recaptured Constantinople in 1261, the city never recovered from the pillage of the Crusaders, weakening it for later conquest by the Turks.

The Ottoman Turks

The Ottoman state began as a tiny principality under the Seljuk Turks in the distant northeastern corner of Anatolia. Benefiting from the rivalries of other Turkish princes and weaknesses of the Byzantine state, however, the Ottomans unified Turks across the Anatolian plateau, and also succeeded in conquering the Balkans, surrounding Constantinople and the remaining territories of the Empire with their grand armies.

On 29 May 1453, Ottoman Sultan Mehmet II was the first to breach the Theodosian walls, bringing an end to the Byzantine Empire. The last Byzantine emperor, Constantine IX, was killed defending the city. Constantinople was renamed Istanbul, derived either from its popular Greek name, Istanopolis, meaning 'to the city', or from the Turkish expression Islambol, which translates as 'where Muslims are plentiful'.

Mehmet the Conqueror's first act was to dedicate Aya Sofya to Allah, turning it into a mosque in the process, but he also began work on Topkapı Palace, the Covered Bazaar and several other mosque complexes. In a short time Istanbul became a fabulously wealthy capital of a different sort, constructed with the Muslim religion, as well as international trade, in mind.

The Ottoman Empire reached its zenith during the Sultanate of Süleyman the Magnificent (1522–66). It was a state both multi-cultural and multi-lingual, whose borders stretched from the gates of Vienna in the west to the tips of the Arab peninsula in the east, and from the Crimea in the north to the Sudan in the south. During his reign, Süleyman had public baths, religious schools and grand mosque complexes erected in the city, including the magnificent Süleymaniye, built by the master architect Sinan.

After Süleyman's death, however, the Ottoman Empire began to decline, and its borders to contract. Due, in part, to a *fatwah* on the printing press along with other scientific advancements, waves of nationalist uprising throughout Ottoman lands, and a string of disastrous military defeats against a new foe in the north – Tsarist Russia – the Ottoman economy stagnated, and ultimately sold out to western powers for industrial aid.

Another setback was the Janissaries, an elite army corps of Christian converts that had degenerated into a mutinous force of its own. In 1826, Sultan Mahmut II disbanded the corps and designed a new military unit, modelled on the armies of Napoleon. As part of this trend towards Europeanisation, Mahmut's son, Sultan Abdül Mecit (1839–1867) built

Left: crusaders attack Constantinople in 1204

the sub-Rococo Dolmabahçe Palace along the Bosphorus at cruel expense to the state. Succeeded by a brother, Abdul Aziz, whose self indulgence stretched to a harem of many thousands, the great days of the Sultans came to a whimpering end when the last true autocrat, Abdül Hamid, retreated within the walls of Yıldız Palace, and the 'Sick Man of Europe' faced his death bed.

The Turks made the fatal mistake of siding with the Central Powers during World War I, their only victory being the tragic slaughter at Gallipoli. After defeat, the Allies carved up the remains of the Ottoman Empire. The French occupied southeast Anatolia, Italian troops landed in Antalya, and Greek forces invaded Izmir, marching east towards Ankara. The British took Istanbul, the Bosphorus and the Dardanelles, and the remains of their occupation, which can be seen in buildings around the Galata Tower today, are still referred to as 'the British Post Office' and 'the British Jail'.

From 1919 to 1922, the Turks, under World War I hero General Mustafa Kemal, fought for independence, vanquishing all occupying forces. The Turkish Republic was founded in 1923 by this still greatly revered leader, who took the name Atatürk, or 'Father of the Turks'.

Westernising Reforms

Atatürk immediately carried out a series of radical reforms intended to bring the new Republic into line with western countries. He abolished the Sultanate and Caliphate, moved the capital from Istanbul to Ankara, and replaced the Sharia, Islamic holy law, with civil, trade and penal codes adopted from the Swiss, French and Italians. He gave women the right to vote and run for elective office, encouraged them to compete with men in every profession and gave them equality before the law. The old Ottoman script, based on Arabic and Persian, was replaced by the Latin alphabet. Surnames were invented and Turks were strongly urged to dispose of the fez, veil and *shalvar* in favour of modern European dress.

In Atatürk's time, Istanbul's influence was insignificant compared to Ankara's. Under his successors, massive government incentives encouraged Turkish businessmen to turn Istanbul into a major industrial and trade centre. Hundreds of new factories along the Golden Horn and shores of the Sea of Marmara provided jobs for an influx of Anatolian peasantry. Since 1945 the population has exploded from 900,000 to more than 12 million, and continues to grow at the rate of up to 500,000 a year, placing a serious strain on the infrastructure, as witnessed by the August 1999 earthquake. According to the Municipality, nearly nine out of ten people in the city today are first-generation peasants,

Right: miniature of Süleyman the Magnificent

and more than 65 percent of the population are aged under 25, with new music venues and fashion outlets opening, and espresso bars and cyber-cafés on every street corner. The yearly Istanbul International Film, Theatre, Music and Jazz Festivals are breaking all attendance records. There is also increasing concern about pollution. The Golden Horn has been cleared of its malodorous waste, formerly derelict areas have become public parks and luxury housing developments, and a multi-billion dollar sewage treat-ment system is being built to clean the seas. A huge subway project begin-ning at Taksim Square is easing traffic congestion in the new town.

Political Backlash

Allegations of corruption in the major political parties, continuing war with the Kurdish separatists in eastern Turkey, and the increasing gap between rich and poor led, in the 1990s, to a rise in support for both the Islamic fundamentalist parties and ultra-right nationalists, the MHP. With the capture of PKK leader Abdullah Öcalan, however, and the watchful eyes of the EU on his sentencing, combined with bust-ups of Hizbollah terrorist strongholds around the country, it was hoped that political extremism in Turkey was coming to an end. The invasion of neighbour-ing Iraq was financially damaging to Turkey, and in 2003 four devastat-ing Al Qaeda bombs were aimed at Jewish and British targets in central Istanbul. Since then, both Kurdish separatists and Al Qaeda have tar-geted the city, but tourists have not been deterred; visitor numbers have reached record levels.

Sympathy generated by the 1999 earthquake tragedy helped to improve relations with the EU member states while IMF aid agreements have ef-fectively mobilised much-needed social reforms. The currency has been revalued to bring it roughly into line with the euro and the dollar, and the country's economy is currently one of the fastest growing in the world. However, the dispute with Greece over Cyprus is unresolved and Turkey remains on the long, long road to possible EU membership.

Above: the Old City

HISTORY HIGHLIGHTS

666BC Megarian leader Byzas establishes Byzantium at the confluence of the Golden Horn, the Bosphorus and the Sea of Marmara.

512 Persian domination of the city begins. Darius builds a bridge of boats in an unsuccessful bid to conquer eastern Europe.

479 Greek rule returns to Byzantium under Pausanias of Sparta.

279 Byzantium repulses invasion by the Celts, but agrees to pay tribute.

179 Rhodes, Pergamum and Bithynia join forces to conquer city. Byzantium becomes part of the Roman Empire.

AD193 Roman Emperor Septimius Severus sacks Byzantium for siding with his rivals in a civil war, though he rebuilds the city and names it Augusta Antonina in honour of his son.

330 Roman Emperor Constantine builds his new capital in the city and names it Constantinople, beginning the Byzantine era.

532 Emperor Justinian stamps out the Nika revolt. More than 30,000 people are killed in a one-day bloodbath, and much of the city is torched.

726 Emperor Leo III smashes a mosaic icon of Christ over Palace entry, provoking a riot. Iconoclasm declared state policy.

787 The Council of Nicaea restores iconolatry.

7th and 8th centuries Arab invaders besiege Constantinople but fail to breach the walls of the city.

1071 Seljuk Turks defeat Byzantines at Malazgirt and sweep into Anatolia, triggering the Crusades.

1204 Christian crusaders sack Constantinople and establish a Latin kingdom in the city.

1261 Byzantine rule of Constantinople restored.

1453 Ottoman Turks conquer Constantinople and name it Istanbul.

16th century Ottoman rule reaches zenith under Süleyman the Magnificent, borders extend from the gates of Vienna to North Africa.

17th century Ottoman Empire begins slow 300-year decline as a result of military defeats, changes in trade routes and failure to keep up with technological advances taking place in western Europe.

1826 Sultan Mahmut II disbands Janissary Corps and builds new military force modelled on Napoleon's army.

1914–1918 Ottoman Empire sides with Germany and Austria-Hungary during World War I.

1919–1922 Istanbul occupied by the Allied forces. The Turks, under Mustafa Kemal, engage in War of Independence.

1923 The Independent Republic of Turkey is established, with a new capital in Ankara. Mustafa Kemal, later known as Atatürk, becomes first President of the Republic.

1920s and 1930s Atatürk carries out sweeping reforms.

1938 Atatürk dies in Istanbul.

1952 Turkey joins NATO.

1945–1991 Istanbul becomes a major industrial centre.

1995 Customs Union agreement signed with EU.

1998 Kurdish separatists (the PKK) begin an armed insurrection in southeastern Turkey; Istanbul suffers intermittent bomb attacks.

August 17, 1999 Istanbul earthquake; thousands perish and up to US$3 billion worth of damage done.

2003 Iraq War. Al Qaeda targets Istanbul with bombs at two synagogues, the British Consulate and HSBC Bank.

2005 Start of formal talks on making Turkey a member of the EU.

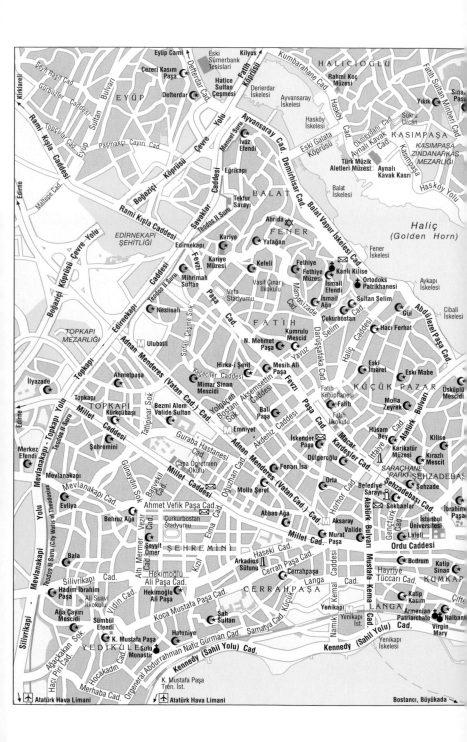

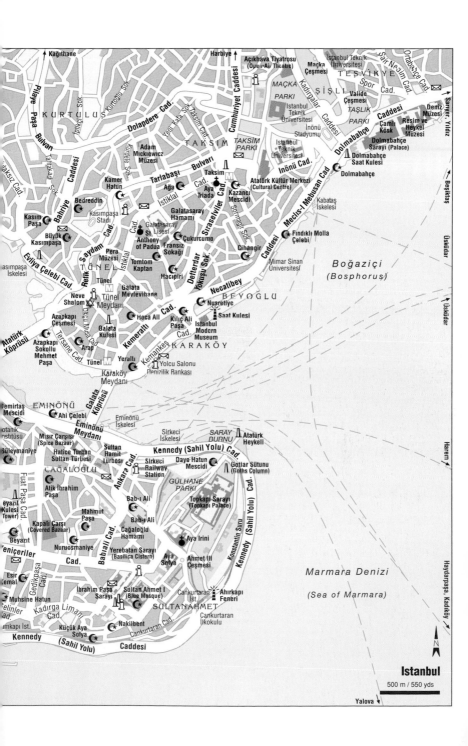

Istanbul

500 m / 550 yds

City Itineraries

Istanbul, one of the world's largest cities, is a vast, skinny metropolis stretching more than 50km (32 miles) along the Bosphorus to the Marmara Sea. With more than 500 mosques, 150 churches and synagogues, a dozen palaces, ancient bazaars and hundreds more historic monuments, it is one of the most colourful cities on the planet. But for the short-stay visitor, the main attractions are around the triangular peninsula between the Golden Horn and the Sea of Marmara, today referred to as the 'Old City' – the site of Byzantine Constantinople and the Ottoman 'Stamboul'. There are many fine old restored houses and even small mansions in the area of Sultanahmet, near the Blue Mosque and Topkapı Palace, which have been converted to reasonably-priced hotels and pensions.

The best way to tour Istanbul is to take long, leisurely walks, combined with metro, taxi and *dolmuş* (shared taxi) rides, which are both plentiful and inexpensive. If you find yourself succumbing to fatigue during your strolls, simply stop off at one of the many outdoor coffeehouses that line the main tourist areas, where you may also find the opportunity to smoke a *nargile* or waterpipe full of scented Persian tobacco.

If you decide to cross the Bosphorus, do as most Istanbulites do – take a ferry. It's a great way to escape the summer heat as well as see the stunning skyline without the tourist crush. Avoid making the mistake of renting a car in the city, or if you must, make sure it is chauffeur-driven. With traffic at a standstill much of the time and parking spaces almost non-existent, driving in Istanbul is a waste of precious holiday time.

1. THE OLD CITY *(see map, page 22)*

Begin at Sultanahmet Park. Visit the Blue Mosque, the ancient Hippodrome and the Turkish and Islamic Arts Museum. Explore the Yerebatan Sarayı (Sunken Palace or Basilica Cistern) and have lunch nearby. Reserve the afternoon for the special spiritual atmosphere of Aya Sofya, and finish off with the Turkish Handwoven Carpets Exhibition and a gentle walk down Soğukçeşme.

Start at Sultanahmet Park by 8.30am for a leisurely stroll around the district. This is the traditional religious hub of the city, and you can easily walk to most of the main sites on your first day. It is also a pick-up site for touts; bear this in mind if you are approached by anyone here.

The northeastern end of the park is dominated by **Aya Sofya**, or Haghia Sophia, the justifiably famous 6th-century Byzantine basilica that later became a mosque and is now a

Left: no stone is left uncovered inside the stunning Blue Mosque
Right: tea sellers are a common sight around the city

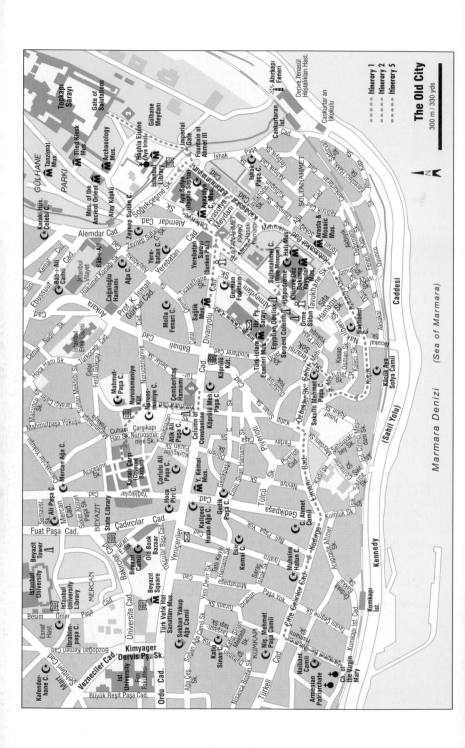

Above Right: a devout Muslim prepares for prayer
Right: the Blue Mosque with the Sea of Marmara beyond

museum. Sultanahmet Camii, better known in the west as the Blue Mosque, stands in the southwest corner, only 180m (200yds) from the church, and is popularly thought to have been built to outshine it.

These two edifices dominate Istanbul's skyline with their piercing minarets and domes – one is among the highest achievements of the Christian world, the other a masterpiece of Islamic architecture. The scant remains of the famous Hippodrome, where chariot races were held during the Byzantine period, is to the west of the park.

The Blue Mosque

It was near this park that Byzas founded Istanbul 27 centuries ago, and where part of the Byzantine Great Palace complex stood, covering the area from the present site of the Blue Mosque down to the Marmara Sea. You can still see traces of this palace behind the mosque and on the sea walls.

The **Blue Mosque (Sultanahmet Camii)** opens for first prayers at 5.30am, and you will gain time by visiting it first. Like other mosques in the city, it is open seven days a week (except during prayers), and closes at 7pm. This is one of the most magnificent shrines in the Muslim world, taking its name from the exquisite blue tiles that cover its interior walls. Built for Ahmet I, who ascended the throne at the age of 12 and reigned from 1603 to 1618, it has six minarets – a controversy at the time and equalled only by El Haram, the mosque that surrounds the Kaaba in Mecca; the architect, Mehmet Aga, was sent to Mecca to add another minaret and preserve its seniority.

Like most imperial religious foundations, the Blue Mosque was the centrepiece of a complex of buildings, known as a *külliye*. In addition to the mosque, the complex included a *medrese* (higher Islamic institute of learning), a *türbe* (tomb of its founder), an *imaret* (public kitchens where food was served to the poor), a hospital, a *caravansarai* (where visiting traders

and businessmen could stay) and a primary school. The hospital and *caravansarai* were destroyed in a 19th-century fire. The public kitchens were located in the administration buildings of Marmara University, which stands at the southern end of the Hippodrome, before they, too, burnt down. Recently restored, the primary school stands above the northeastern entrance.

The *medrese* is located to the right of the northern precinct walls of the mosque and is now used to store some of the documents of the **Ottoman Archives**. Next to it is the **Tomb of Ahmet I** (9.30am–4.30pm, closed Mon and Tue), who was only 27 years old when he died. Buried next to him are his wife, Köşem Sultan, and his three sons, Osman II (sultan 1618–22), Murat IV (sultan 1623–40), Prince Beyazıt, and their relations. All are covered by dark green fabric, the universal colour of Islam, and each male grave has a turban-shaped tombstone.

Köşem Sultan, one of the most powerful women in the Ottoman state, ruled the Harem and (historians suggest) the Empire, through her husband, two sons and grandson Mehmet IV, for nearly five decades. The daughter of a Greek priest, she entered the harem at 13 and won the heart of Sultan Ahmet with her beauty. Rival factions in the Harem, jealous of her influence over sultans, strangled her with a cord in 1651.

Inside the Mosque

Enter the vast mosque grounds through the northern gateway. The ornate ramp to your immediate left leads to the Hünkar Kasrı, a suite of rooms used by the sultan when he came to pray. These lead into the Hünkar Mahfili, the imperial quarters in the upper gallery of the mosque. The sultan usually attended the main Friday services, riding his white horse into the mosque precinct and up the ramp into his suite (which also had stables), giving the people a chance to see him. Today the sultan's suite houses the **Carpets and Kilims Museum** (renovated in 2007; usually open Tue–Sun 8.30am–5pm), which has a remarkable collection of weavings from more than 200 mosques throughout Turkey, some more than two centuries old.

The Blue Mosque is preceded on the western side by a large rectangular courtyard, or *avlu*, with a monumental gateway on each side. In its midst is an octagonal *şadörvan*, or fountain, where Muslim pre-prayer ablutions once took place. Today, washing is carried out at the taps along the north-

Above: the interior walls of the Blue Mosque are clad in exquisite Iznik tiles.

ern exterior wall of the mosque. From the courtyard, you can get a spectacular view of the cascading domes and half domes of the mosque. The main entrance facing the courtyard is usually reserved for Muslims coming to pray. Tourists are asked to enter through the northern door when prayers have finished. Always remove your shoes when entering a mosque, and wear appropriate clothing. Women must cover hair and arms; scarves are usually available at the door. Offering a small donation for upkeep of the mosque is standard practise on departure. The main prayers are at noon on Friday when 25,000 Muslims wearing white skullcaps cram its interior to bow down to Allah and listen to the sermon of the *imam* (prayer leader).

Shafts of light penetrate the mosque's 260 windows, many of which are filled with stained glass, producing a kaleidoscope of colours. The walls are covered with 16th-century blue tiles that were produced in the kilns of Iznik, a city in western Anatolia famed for its ceramics. The interior is 51 metres (60yds) by 53 metres (63yds) and its 23-metre (80-ft) dome is supported by four 'elephant-feet' columns and half domes.

The Ancient Hippodrome

As you leave the Blue Mosque through the monumental gateway in the front courtyard, you come to **At Meydanı**, the ancient Hippodrome, which was the centre of civic affairs during the Byzantine era. In 203 Roman Emperor Septimius Severus began construction of the gigantic stadium, which was completed during the reign of Constantine the Great. In addition to weekly chariot races and gladiatorial combats, it was a forum for the city's rival Green and Blue factions, whose support the Emperor desperately needed to retain power. It was in the Hippodrome, in January 532, that Justinian's generals suppressed the Nika revolt, with some 30,000 insurgents killed.

Little remains of the stadium except for three monuments in the middle of the Hippodrome. The **Egyptian Obelisk** or **Dikilitaş** is perhaps the most impressive. Commissioned by Pharaoh Thutmose III (1549–1503BC) and erected originally at Deir el Bahri, opposite Thebes in upper Egypt, the 26-metre (84-ft) monument commemorates one of Thutmose's campaigns in Syria and his crossing of the Euphrates River. Constantine the Great brought the 800-tonne obelisk to Constantinople in the 4th century, though it was mounted by his successor, Theodosius the Great. Standing on four brazen blocks resting on a marble base, the reliefs on four sides depict the Emperor Theodosius watching chariot races with his wife, crowning the victors, assisting in the mounting of the Obelisk, and receiving supplication from vanquished enemies.

The second of the original monuments in the Hippodrome is the **Serpent Column** of three intertwined bronze snakes. The

Right: elaborate attention to detail in the Blue Mosque

heads fell off, purportedly during one of the circus riots. These serpents formed the base of a trophy that once stood in the Temple of Apollo at Delphi, dedicated to Apollo in appreciation of his support of the Greeks in their victory over the Persians at the Battle of Plataea in 479BC. It was also brought to the city by Constantine.

Little is known about the 32-metre (105-ft) **Column of Constantine Porphryogenitus** (Ormetaş) other than it was once covered in bronze, which was later carried off by crusaders. In Ottoman times, Jannissary soldiers used it for scaling practise. The final monument in the Hippodrome is the **Fountain of Kaiser Wilhelm II**, known today as the **German Fountain** or **Alman Çeşmesi**, built in 1898 to commemorate the German Kaiser's second visit to Istanbul. It stood as a symbol of the growing influence of Germany in Turkey during the last years of the Ottoman Empire, which sided with the Central Powers during World War I.

Turkish and Islamic Art

Ibrahim Paşa Sarayı (Palace), on the Hippodrome opposite the Blue Mosque, contains the **Museum of Turkish and Islamic Arts** (9.30am–4.30pm, closed Mon; entrance fee), considered to be one of the best museums in Turkey as well as one of the finest Ottoman residential buildings in Istanbul. A Greek convert to Islam, Ibrahim Paşa was a close friend of the sultan and was married to Süleyman's sister Hatice, which explains the grandeur of his palace as well as its proximity to Topkapı. But Ibrahim Paşa's influence over the sultan roused the ire of other courtiers, including the sultan's favourite wife, Hürrem Sultan (Roxelana), who conspired to have him strangled in 1536. Such was the fate of many Grand Viziers (a total of 15 out of 17 met a violent death between 1644 and 1656), inspiring the Ottoman saying: 'The neck of a servant of the sultan is thinner than a hair's breadth.'

The museum contains more than 40,000 items dating from the earliest period of Islam under the Omayyad caliphate (661–750), specialising in religious artefacts and historic carpets, with particular reference to the use of Turkish carpets in paintings by European masters such as Holbein. A pleasant, traditional Ottoman-style coffeehouse on the ground floor serves tea and genuine Turkish coffee in a large garden that overlooks the Hippodrome.

Walk back to Sultanahmet Park, and when you come to the end, cross the busy street and tram line known as **Divanyolu**, the **Council Avenue**, where many imperial parades were held during both Byzantine and Ottoman times. You'll see the **Bust of Halide Edip Adıvar**, a distinguished woman novelist and nationalist who played a key role in the Turkish War of Independence. At the corner of the square is the entrance to the remarkable **Yerebatan Sarayı**, or **Sunken Palace** (daily 9am–4pm; closed Mon; entrance fee). This is not

Above: an elderly man relaxes in the ancient Hippodrome

really a palace, however, but the **Basilica Cistern**, one of 18 water storage facilities built during the Byzantine period. Initiated by Constantine and later expanded by Justinian in 532, it supplied the considerable needs of the Royal Palace complex. The lack of fresh water was always a problem in early Constantinople, and plagues were almost continuous as a result.

The cistern is some 70 metres (77yds) wide and 140 metres (155yds) in length, with a total of 336 columns arranged in 12 rows of 28, many of which were probably pilfered from pre-Christian temples – note the Medusa heads at the base of two of them, one on its side, near the back exit. The cistern was capable of holding enough water to sustain part of the city during a long siege. Water was pumped in from a reservoir near the Black Sea, 19km (12 miles) from Istanbul, through a series of aqueducts.

Underground Cathedral

Today, the cistern is a unique attraction, cool on the hottest of days – a dark and cleverly-lit underground chamber with a vast, cathedral-like ceiling. Bridges and walkways have been constructed over the water and you can walk along illuminated promenades listening to strains of Bach and Mozart. A spectacular scene from the James Bond film *From Russia With Love* was staged

here, and it is also used to great effect during Istanbul's acclaimed art biennial. Just outisde stands the **Milion**, the marker from which all distances in the empire were measured.

For a real treat walk a short distance along Divanyolu and look to the left for the the **Binbirdirek Sarnıcı** (Cistern of 1001 Columns; open daily 9am–6pm), another beautifully restored Byzantine cistern that has an excellent restaurant, café, *nargile* bar and craft stalls.

You may also cross the tramway in the direction of Aya Sofya and take a short detour along **Alemdar Caddesi** to **Caferağa Medresesi** (9am–7pm), a 16th-century theological school now serving as a teahouse and handicraft centre. The rectangular *medrese* was constructed by Mimar Sinan (1497–1588), the most famous Ottoman architect. A

Above: Medusa head in the Basilica Cistern. **Right:** the Cistern's columns

contemporary of Michelangelo, Sinan served as chief architect to the court from 1538 to 1588. According to art historian Aptullah Kuran, Sinan built 477 mosques, *medreses*, Turkish Baths and bridges, of which 319 are in Istanbul. At the handicraft centre, courses are given in traditional Turkish arts, including *hüsn-i hat* (calligraphy), *ebru* (paper marbling), the making of meerschaum pipes, miniatures, stained glass, jewellery and carpets, all of which can be purchased here.

Aya Sofya

Aya Sofya (the Church of Divine Wisdom, also known as Haghia Sophia; 9.30am–4.30pm, June–Oct 9am–7pm; closed Mon), is unquestionably Istanbul's finest site, despite suffering tragically from decay, damp and lack of funds for its upkeep. Ottoman architects, including Sinan, later emulated Aya Sofya in their construction of imperial mosques, attempting to surpass its magnificence. The basilica, which served as the Patriarchal church during the Byzantine era, is best known for its vast interior, high dome and fabulous mosaics, many dating from the 10th century. Mosaics from earlier periods were probably destroyed during the Iconoclastic Movement of the 8th and 9th centuries.

The present basilica is the third imperial church to stand on the site. The first was erected in AD360 during the reign of Roman Emperor Constantius, son and successor of Constantine the Great. Earthquakes, fires and riots caused it to be rebuilt numerous times until Justinian the Great created the final structure in 537. When Mehmet II conquered the city, his first stop was Aya Sofya, which he immediately declared a mosque and dedicated to Allah. Apart from chipping away some of the marble crosses, he left the church much as it was, simply whitewashing the mosaic icons and hanging the huge wooden medallions with Islamic inscriptions. The four minarets at the corners were added at various times after the Turkish conquest.

In 1935, Kemal Atatürk, founder of the modern Turkish Republic, declared Aya Sofya a museum in order to quell any further debate over to whom it really belonged, and museum authorities restored many of the mosaics. Along with Ephesus, a Hellenistic city on the Aegean coast, this is the most popular site in the country, attracting more than 2 million visitors every year. Unfortunately, the controversy over whether it is church or mosque still surfaces from time to time. When Pope John Paul II visited in 1979 and said a prayer,

Above: Koranic inscriptions converted Aya Sofya to a mosque
Right: elegantly piled domes make Aya Sofya one of the world's greatest landmarks

Islamic fundamentalists were incensed, and soon afterwards a group of fanatical Muslim students burst in and held their own prayers.

The courtyard has many Byzantine relics, including columns, statues and sarcophagi, that have been unearthed in different parts of the city. The main entrance to the church, in the southwest corner, is now used as the exit. This was the Imperial Gate, used by emperors. In Byzantine times it was widely believed that the massive door was made from the wood of Noah's Ark.

A Reflection of Heaven

Entrance to the church is now through the grand western doors. Just above the portal leading to the interior is a stunning mosaic depicting Christ seated on a jewelled throne. In his left hand he holds a book inscribed, 'Peace be with you. I am the Light of the World.' On Christ's right, Emperor Leo VI (886–912) prostrates himself, his hands stretched out, as if pleading forgiveness. Two medallions above show the Virgin Mary and the archangel Gabriel. The mosaic, historians say, depicts the emperor asking Christ for permission to take a fourth wife, usually forbidden by the Orthodox Church.

From the outer vestibule, you enter the immense interior, covering an area of 7,570 sq metres (1.85 acres). It is noted for its ethereal, heavenly quality, dominated by the massive dome easily seen from every part of the church. Ancient historians described it as appearing ominously suspended from heaven by a golden chain. Four gigantic piers support the dome, which stands 56 metres (183ft) above the floor. The east–west diameter of the dome is 31 metres (102ft) and the north–south diameter is 33 metres (108ft).

To the left of the entrance is the 'sweating column' where Justinian cured his migraine by resting his forehead on the cool stone. Women in search of a husband should put their fingers in the deeply worn holes and twist their hand 360°. Towards the front, the floor is marked by the point on which the Emperor had his throne, the official centre of the Byzantine world.

city itineraries

The most fascinating mosaic in the nave has survived in the conch of the apse (the eastern side of the building). It depicts the Virgin Mary with the Christ-child on her knee. The child is dressed in gold, his right hand held out in blessing. In his left hand he holds a scroll. At the bottom of the arch which frames the apse is the colossal figure of the archangel Gabriel with his fluffy, brightly-coloured feathers. On the north side of the arch, opposite the mosaic, you can see a few sad remaining feathers of the archangel Michael. The other mosaics in the interior are located in niches at the base of the north tympanum wall, representing the three saints: St Ignatius the Younger, St John Chrysostom and St Ignatius Theophorus.

The only other mosaics in the interior are the famous six-winged seraphim or cherubim in the eastern pendentives. Those in the western pendentives are imitations, the work of the Swiss Fossati brothers who were involved in the 1847–49 restorations. The gigantic wooden medallions added by the Turks after the conquest are inscribed with the names of Allah, Mohammed, the first caliphs and the first two *imams* of the mosque. The Turks also added a *mihrap*, a prayer niche, to the south side of the apse indicating the direction of Mecca, a *mimber*, or stepped pulpit from which the *imam* led the congregation in prayer, and the ornate sultan's box to the left of the apse.

Gallery Mosaics

You can find the the remaining mosaics in the upper galleries, reached by staircases opening into the outer vestibule. Only one is in the northern gallery: that of Byzantine Emperor Alexander (912–13) in his ceremonial robe and crown of gold adorned with pearls. In the south gallery are several mosaics: one shows Empress Zöe and her third husband, Constantine IX Monomachos. At the centre of the composition is Christ, his right hand raised in a gesture of benediction; in his left hand he holds the Bible. To his left is the emperor, offering a bag of money. The empress is to his right, holding a scroll. Married several times to weak sovereigns, Zöe ruled the empire from behind the scenes.

The mosaic known as the **Deesis** is the finest. Although parts of it are lost, the features of the three figures remain intact, with Christ flanked by the Virgin and St John the Baptist, who are leaning toward Christ, as if pleading for the salvation of mankind. Set into the pavement across from the Deesis is the **Tomb of Henricus Dandalo**, the Doge of Venice and one of the leaders of the Fourth Crusade. Dandalo was responsible for the sack of Constantinople in 1204, when the Catholic crusaders killed thousands of Orthodox Christians and established a Latin kingdom in the city. It is said that after the Byzantines recovered the city in 1261, mobs broke into the despot's tomb and tossed his bones to the dogs. The last mosaic is situated over

Left: Byzantine mosaic of Christ, one of many in Aya Sofya

the vestibule door before the exit and shows the enthroned Virgin Mary holding the Christ-child in her lap as the Emperor Constantine the Great presents her with a model of the city, while Emperor Justinian offers her a model of Aya Sofya.

Five Ottoman sultans and their families are buried in the precincts of Aya Sofya but the royal *türbes*, or mausoleums, are not open to visitors. Monarchs buried here include Mustafa I, who ruled briefly from 1617–18 and again in1622–3, Ibrahim the Mad (1640–8), and Selim the Sot, the alcoholic son of Süleyman the Magnificent (1566–74). Selim died at the age of 54, supposedly after suffering a fall in the bath house. Besides Selim's catafalque is his favourite wife, Nurbanu, and the tombs of his five sons, three of his daughters and 32 children of his eldest son and successor, Murat III (1574–95). Upon Selim's death his other sons were murdered to allow the peaceful succession of Murat.

The Price of Power

Murat's own *türbe* stands just beside that of his father. The night Murat died, 19 of his sons were killed to allow his eldest son, Mehmet III (1595–1603), to inherit the throne. This was the last occasion that fratricide was practised in determining the sultan, though other cruel methods took its place in the following years.

Directly across Aya Sofya Square, the **Haseki Hürrem Hamamı** – a bath house built by Sinan in 1556 for Roxelana, the wife of Süleyman the Magnificent – is now home to the state-run **Turkish Handwoven Carpets Exhibition** (9am–4.30pm, closed Sun and Mon) with expert staff and reasonable prices; even of you are not interested in carpets it is worth having a look at the interior of the building. The monumental entrance to the Byzantine Great Palace once stood to the left of the *hamam*.

Return to the entrance to the bath and walk straight along the eastern walls of Aya Sofya. Just before the entrance to Topkapı Palace is the **Fountain of Ahmet III**, constructed in the early 18th century, and on the left is **Soğukçeşme Sokak**, a narrow street lined with restored pastel-coloured houses, now the **Aya Sofya Pensions** (Aya Sofya Pansiyonları, see page 99), a pleasant hotel complex. The **Istanbul Library** (Mon, Wed and Fri, for research) is also in the same street. With 6,000 volumes, it has the best collection of books on Istanbul in the world. A large cistern alongside the houses is now a taverna, the **Sarnıç**, (or **Cistern Restaurant**), where excellent Ottoman-style lunches and dinners are served.

Above: Aya Sofya's awe-inspiring dome

2. TOPKAPI PALACE *(see maps, below and page 22)*

Tour of Topkapı Palace; lunch in the palace complex overlooking the sea; afternoon tea at Yeşil Ev; see the remains of the Byzantine Great Palace in the Mosaic Museum; walk down to Küçük Aya Sofya Camii and Sokullu Mehmet Paşa Camii; visit the Armenian Church Patriarchate; dinner in Kumkapı.

You can easily spend a full day exploring **Topkapı Palace** (9am–7pm, June–Oct 9am–7pm, closed Tue; separate entrance fees for the main palace, treasury and harem) and its various courts. But with a well-planned and structured visit you can see the most important sites within three or four hours, and even have lunch. Bring your own cold drinks, and book your harem tickets (available only at harem entrance) once inside. Tours fill up quickly and the last is at 4pm. Try to leave time for the government-run gift shop, Dösem, on your way out as it has an interesting selection, reasonable prices and no high-pressure salesmanship.

For almost 400 years, Topkapı Palace was the residence of the Ottoman sultans, some of the most powerful rulers in the world. As their armies rushed from conquest to conquest, from within Topkapı's

Topkapı Palace
100 m / 110 yds

GÜLHANE PARKI

Pool
Bağdat Köşkü
Sofa Köşkü (Mustafa Paşa Pavilion)
Circumcision Room
Fourth Court
Revan Köşkü
Mecidiye Köşkü
Hırka-i Saadet (Pavilion of the Holy Mantle)
Collection of Calligraphy, Miniatures and Manuscripts
Kiler Odası (Hall of the Pantry)
HAREM GARDEN
Harem
Library
Third Court
Library of Ahmet III
Treasury
İç Hazine (Inner Treasury)
Arz Odası (Throne Room)
Clock Room
Baba-ı Sa'adet (Gate of Felicity)
Imperial Costumes Exhibition
Imperial Stables
Council Chamber
Second Court
Palace Kitchens
Bab-üs Selam (Gate of Salutations)
First Court
Ticket Office

Above: Topkapı's imposing Imperial Gate leads to the First Court

walls the sultans ruled a vast empire that stretched, in its heyday, from the gates of Vienna to the Indian Ocean, and from North Africa to the Crimean Peninsula. A city within a city, Topkapı Palace consists of interconnecting courts and groups of buildings reflecting the feudal lifestyle of the nomadic Ottoman warriors. Anywhere between 4,000 and 7,000 people worked and lived inside it, serving the imperial household.

The Harem is often cited as a reason for the eventual downfall of the empire; many historians, however, believe that it was the Ottoman dynasty's obscure rules of succession – leading to fratricide on a massive scale – as well as the later institution of the *Kafes* or Cage (*Veliaht Dairesi*), which led to the execution of many able statesmen and princes, that contributed to the slow decay and eventual collapse of the Ottoman Empire. By the 19th century, the palace had come to symbolise the 'sick man of Europe', and even the last of the sultans had abandoned it.

Topkapı, which means Cannon Gate, gets its name from the two cannons that stood by its sea walls. The Venetians, who fought against the Ottomans for many centuries, described it as the Seraglio of the Grand Signor. But to the Turks it was simply the Saray, a Persian word meaning palace. It is located on the first hill of the old city, settled since pre-Christian times, and encompasses the promontory known as **Saray Burnu** (Palace Point), at the confluence of the Sea of Marmara, the Bosphorus and the Golden Horn. Today, a modern highway and railway run along the shore through parts of what were formerly the outer gardens.

Mehmet's Crowning Glory

Mehmet the Conqueror's first palace, in 1453, was on the third hill of the city, where Istanbul University stands today. But his growing retinue required a larger residence, and he moved to Topkapı in the mid-1470s, leaving the old Palace, long gone, to become the final pastures of the harems of deceased or deposed sultans and elderly servants.

Mahmut II (1808–39) was the last sultan to reside at Topkapı. He wished to promote a more European-style image, and built Dolmabahçe Palace along the Bosphorus, nearly bankrupting the state. One of the last sultans, Abdülhamit II (1876–1909), constructed a third palace at today's Yıldız Park, also along the Bosphorus. In 1924, one year after the proclamation of the Turkish Republic and the abolition of the sultanate, Topkapı Palace was declared a museum.

The main entrance to the Topkapı is through the **Imperial Gate**, or Bab-ı-Hümayün, just opposite the Fountain of Ahmet III. It leads to the First Court, also known as the **Court of the Janissaries**. Above the gate you can see the *tuğra*, or emblem, of Mahmut II. The inscriptions above the *tuğra* are of Mehmet II, the sultan who conquered the city and built Topkapı. The Imperial Gate was always open to the public, as now, but was guarded by sentries, who would shut its massive doors only in times of anti-

Right: facing a bright future

government disturbances. Sometimes, when riots occurred, these sentries connived with the mobs outside, allowing them to burst into the palace, seize an unpopular grand vizier or sultan, and execute him on the spot.

Today, the long First Court is a public park lined with flowers, plane trees and tour buses, but during the Ottoman period state processions began and

ended here, especially on Fridays when the sultan went to pray in one of the imperial mosques. The First Court also housed offices and buildings of a more public and practical nature, and was the assembly point for those petitioning the **Divan** in the second court. Once inside, however, a strict rule of silence was imposed.

Aya Irini

To the left as you walk through the court is the city's earliest Byzantine church, **Aya Irini**, the Church of St Eirene. Originally constructed by Constantine the Great in the 4th century, it served as the Patriarchal cathedral until the completion of Aya Sofya. The Ottomans used it as an arsenal, and today it is open for special exhibitions and choral concerts during the Istanbul Music Festival in June. Next to it is the **Imperial Mint**, or Darphane. If either building is open, it's worth taking a glimpse inside.

Near the ticket office and gift shop stands the **Cellât Çeşmesi** (or Executioner's Fountain), which was used to wash blood off swords and hands. Executions were among the many duties of the palace gardeners. White columns nearby were called the **Warning Stones**, as they held the detached heads of important offenders. The heads, tongues or noses of lesser criminals were stuck in niches on the outside of the Imperial Gate.

The Inner Sanctum

The inner palace consists of three primary courts. These would have led to other courtyards, pavilions and halls and were connected by a maze of gates and paths, a city within a city, complete with dormitories for various guards, craftsmen and gardeners, all wearing their own distinctively coloured garb. Like a tent city, which it very much resembles, each pavilion served a separate purpose and each new sultan added his own.

Entry to the **Second Court** is through the **Gate of Salutations** or the Bab-ı-Selam. Its two towers, resembling conical witches hats, were used as dungeons to imprison candidates for the Executioner's Fountain. The gate opens onto what was once a splendid garden full of exotic birds and animals, where ceremonial processions and state banquets were held. To the immediate right are miniature models of Topkapı Palace as it was during the 16th century. Take the lane that leads diagonally to the right, leading to the doors of the **Palace Kitchens**, a series of rooms now displaying the Collection of Chinese, Japanese and European Porcelains brought to sultans

Above: Aya Irini is one of the the oldest Christian shrines in Istanbul
Right: palace porcelain and miniature paintings depicting Ottoman life

via the Silk Road. In these kitchens, food was cooked for up to 20,000 people daily, and a reproduction complete with huge cauldrons and other cooking utensils can be seen in the room furthest to the northeast.

China, Silver and Crystal

Two of the chambers show 4,584 pieces of Ming and Ch'ing dynasty porcelain from a collection of more than 10,000 gathered by the sultans over the years. The celadon (green-coloured dishes) were an early form of Chinese porcelain that was believed to change colour if poisoned food was placed on them. Iznik pottery on the other hand, was considered common, fit only for the servants and Janissaries.

In the chambers across from the porcelain collections, you can see the **Silver and Crystal Collection**, of which the most interesting item is a miniature model of the Fountain of Ahmet III, in silver and brass. The southernmost chambers house the **Topkapı Archives**, which has a good collection of original documents and manuscripts from the early Ottoman Empire, although it is open only to researchers. The northernmost room contains the Istanbul Porcelain and Glassware, which came from a factory established by Abdül Hamit II on the grounds of Yıldız Palace. The collection of colourful glassware known as **Nightingale's Eyes** is valued at several million dollars.

Cross the Second Court to the İç Hazine, or **Inner Treasury**, in the northeastern corner, where the Janissaries were paid. It is now home to an exhibition of **Arms and Armour** which includes 400 weapons from various Muslim Empires, dating from the 7th to the 20th centuries, including helmets, shields, swords, rifles, blunderbusses, armour, pistols and *tugs* (horse-tails which were emblems of rank). The most interesting item is the **Sword of Mehmet the Conqueror**, with its gold-engraved inscriptions.

The Conference Room

The adjacent enclosure with three domed rooms just south of the armoury is the **Divan**, or Kubbe Altı (Hall Under the Dome) where the Imperial Council met four times a week, reclining on cushioned benches (divans) At the peak of empire the Divan was one of the most powerful policy-making centres of Europe. The **Council Chamber** was where the grand vizier held periodic meetings with his *divan*, or cabinet, to determine government policies. Just above the chamber was the cubicle of the sultan, who could listen in through a latticed window and could express his views by banging his fist on the railings and shouting through the open window.

The third gate, the **Gate of Felicity** or Baba-üs Saadet was guarded by the White Eunuchs and leads to the **Throne Room** or Arz Odası, where the sultan sat on ceremonial occasions and received viziers after sessions in the Divan. The canopied throne dates from 1596, but there are others in each room of the **Treasury**, including the **Throne of Ahmet III**, inlaid with tortoiseshell and mother-of-pearl set with rubies and emeralds, and another of solid gold. A highlight of the museum, the Treasury is also home to the Ottoman collection of jewels and precious metals, including a diamond-encrusted suit of chain mail, the 18th-century Topkapı dagger, set with huge emeralds, and the 84-carat Spoonmaker's Diamond.

The exhibition of **Imperial Costumes** is on the far right, in what was the Hall of the Pages who looked after the royal wardrobe. Costume was one of early Istanbul's biggest industries, and by the mid 16th century there were 268 looms, a third of them connected to the palace. The buildings surrounding the court were once part of the famous **Palace School**, where young Christian boys, taken from their families

Above: the Imperial Hall
Left: ivory throne in the Treasury

as a kind of tax levy and converted to Islam, were trained to become administrators of the empire. The most able youths rose to the ranks of grand vizier, *kaputan derya* (grand admiral of the fleet), provincial governor or *beylerbeyi*, a supreme governor of an entire region of the empire. The young pages learned Arabic in order to read the Koran, and also learned to read and write the Ottoman script. In addition to these disciplines they had to learn a trade, just in case they should fall from the sultan's favour and be expelled from the palace.

Maps and Miniatures

Just behind the Throne Room is the **Library of Ahmet III**, which resembles a mosque with a dome and raised portico. It is still used to house important palace manuscripts. The Topkapı collection of **Miniatures, Manuscripts and Calligraphy** is at the back, with some works dating to the 12th century. The 16th-century miniatures here convey a good indication of what life was like under the sultans. One of the most interesting relics is the remarkable **Map of Piri Reis**, showing the eastern half of the Americas. The 1513 map was drawn on a piece of gazelle hide and based on Christopher Columbus's lost map. Piri Reis (1465–1555) was a prominent geographer and grand admiral of the Ottoman fleet. His map continues to confound geographers as it was made only a decade after Columbus's voyages, when it was still unclear that Columbus had discovered a new continent.

The art form favoured by the Ottomans, and which escaped the disdain of the clergy was *husn-i hat,* a form of calligraphy thought to come directly from Allah to the scribes' hand. Likewise, the **Collection of European Clocks** was greatly prized by the sultans as Islam forbids the telling of time except for the daily calls to prayer.

Sacred Relics

Most extraordinary, however, is the **Pavilion of the Holy Mantle** containing some of the holiest relics of the Muslim world. Most were acquired by Selim the Grim (1512–20) after the acquisition of Egypt and Syria for the empire and his self-appointment as Caliph, or leader of Islam.

The **Door of Repentance**, taken from the Holy Kaaba in Mecca, dominates the first room, while the second contains Mohammed's footprint and a lock of his hair. An object of particular veneration for Muslims is the **Hırka-i Saadet** or Felicitous Cloak, woven by Mohammed's own harem. Along with the **Sancakçerif** (Sacred Standard), it is kept in gold caskets near two of Mohammed's swords, together with a seal that can only be viewed from an antechamber.

Other relics include hairs of the Prophet's beard and a Holy Tooth. The **Tower of Justice** stands behind the Council Chamber and can be viewed from the court. It was used as a watch tower to ob-

Right: fountain in the library of Ahmet III

serve the city, especially during civil upheavals. Enter the **Fourth Court** (through passageways at the end of the Third Court) to visit the numerous kiosks, or summerhouses and gardens, where the sultans and their favourites relaxed and enjoyed themselves.

Views over the Golden Horn

The left-hand passageway takes you along a corridor of pillars to a water fountain surrounded by three kiosks overlooking Istanbul Harbour and the Golden Horn. These are the **Revan Kiosk**, the **Baghdad Kiosk** and the **Circumcision Room**, or **Sünnet Odası**. The Revan Kiosk was built in 1635 to celebrate the Ottoman capture of the Armenian city of Erivan (Revan) from Persia, and the 17th-century Baghdad Pavilion was a reading room. The Fourth Court has three other summerhouses, the **Kiosk of Kara Mustafa Paşa**, an early 18th-century villa; the **Chamber of the Chief Physician** and the magnificent **Mecidiye Pavilion**, built by Abdul Mecit (sultan 1839–61) in which he would receive guests. The lower floor of the pavilion, which has a stunning patio overlooking the Sea of Marmara, is run by the **Konyalı Restaurant**, where you can have lunch before returning for your harem tour. The prices are moderate and the view is spectacular.

Life in the Harem

The **Harem**, or Forbidden Place, consists of more than 400 rooms, but only about 40 are open to the public. Life inside was not the den of debauchery many westerners imagine and, in fact, bore more relation to a strict convent school than a brothel. The Harem was a complete, self-sustaining unit, consisting of dormitories, private quarters, two small mosques, a school, a swimming pool and baths. Between 500 and 1,500 people lived within its walls, subject to strict discipline and a rigorous hierarchy. Unromantically, it was foremost a breeding pen to provide heirs to the throne by slave mothers

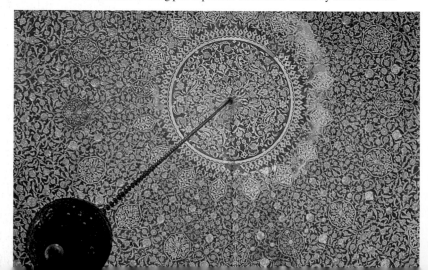

who could not make legal claims of inheritance. In fact, a great deal of Ottoman family law was designed to wriggle through inconsistencies in Islamic canon and explains the later Haseki and Valide Sultan system, which awarded women status if, and only if, they became 'mothers of sultans'.

Some women entered the harem either as war prisoners or slaves purchased through the Slave Market in the Grand Bazaar. But many came willingly, and were groomed for the part, much as a young woman might prepare for a career in Hollywood today. A slave girl's primary goal was to catch the sultan's eye, (*gözde*, literally 'in the eye'), often during demonstrations of musical or dancing abilities, which took place in the **Hünkar Sofrası** (Imperial Hall). She was then bathed and dressed for the occasion, and sent a gift before being led to his own special harem chamber. If she gave birth to a boy, she acquired the elevated status of Haseki Sultan.

Süleyman and Roxelana

By the 18th century it had become difficult to keep control of the harem, which could contain between 400 and 800 women, and the sultans were often reduced to supplying service on a rota basis. The harem had more than 300 rooms, but some were little bigger than prison cubicles.

Some sultans were monogamous and faithful to one of their wives, while others, such as Murat III, were officially credited with as many as 103 offspring from their harems. Süleyman's love for Roxelana, for instance, caused him to break the rules, and their passion for each other is well documented. His decision to move his harem to Topkapı Palace 80 years after the Conquest is generally thought to have been due to her pleading, and she was granted her own sumptuous rooms, as well as space for her entourage of slaves and eunuchs.

Roxelana had four sons, but Süleyman also had a son from an earlier liaison, and a vicious fight between the two women broke out, after which the rival was banished to Bursa, her son strangled, and Roxelana's son Selim 'the Sot' became sultan. Likewise, the 17th century sultan Abdülhamid I became enthralled with a harem favourite named Rühhah, leaving a love note behind which read: 'I am your bound slave, beat me or kill me if you wish. I surrender myself utterly to you.'

Enter the Harem through the **Carriage Gate**, which leads to the **Guard Room** and **Quarters of the Black Eunuchs**. These were up to 200 Sudanese slaves who governed the household. From 1574 until 1908, the chief black eunuch was one of the most powerful men in the palace, being the accountant to the harem as well as disciplinarian. He was also the only man besides the sultan permitted to enter, and his spe-

Top Left: the Baghdad kiosk overlooks the Golden Horn. **Left:** ceiling of the Baghdad kiosk. **Right:** Ottoman miniature of bathtime in the harem

cial privilege and power lay in his access to the throne and his ability to exploit rivalries within his domain.

The next gate, or **Cümle Kapısı**, opens to the **Golden Way**, a path of corridors and courtyards that runs from one end of the Harem to the other. The most powerful woman in the Harem was indisputably the Valide Sultan, or mother of the ruling sultan. Under her were his other wives, concubines and odalisques, along with the servant women. She had her own quarters and eunuchs, as did each wife and favoured concubine. The sultan's children lived in separate chambers, and the Valide Sultan often selected the concubines for her son.

Order of the Bath

Passing the Harem bath house and the Courtyard of the Concubines, you'll reach the **Quarters of the Valide Sultan**, strategically located between the apartments of the Sultan and his higher ranking favourites. It was here that Kÿşem Sultan ruled the empire through her husband, two sons and grandson, before being strangled in 1651 on the orders of her daughter-in-law. Selim III was also murdered here in 1807, though his cousin and successor, Mahmut II, escaped death by hiding in a cupboard.

The next room is the **Sultan's Bath**, entirely furnished in marble and alabaster, followed by the **Room with Fountains**. Murat III used it as a bedroom and for private conversations, turning the taps on to discourage eavesdroppers. The **Sultan's Chamber**, or **Hünkâr Sofrası**, the biggest room in the Harem, is where private pleasures were taken. The **Court of the Favourites** is surrounded by apartments in which each of the sultan's favourite concubines had rooms to herself.

The most interesting room in the Harem is the Veliaht Dairesi, the **Heir's Chambers** – the notorious *Altın Kafes*, or Gilded Cage. Mehmet the Conqueror decreed that whichever of his sons should inherit the throne, it behoved him to kill his brothers 'in the interests of the world order', and in the four centuries of Ottoman rule, 80 princes were killed by strangulation, the preferred method for royalty. Murad III sired 103 children, and at his death 20 sons survived him. But when the eldest, Mehmet III, was called to the throne, his first act as sultan was to murder his 19 brothers and dispose of seven concubines who had been impregnated by his father; their bodies were dumped into the Bosphorus. With royal deaths on such a scale, the courts became concerned about the extinction of the dynasty, and in 1607 fratricide was replaced with the 'Cage' in which male heirs to the throne were kept as pampered prisoners for years, often for life. The throne always went to the

Above: the Harem's Fruit Room, designed to entice Ahmet III to eat
Right: the Room with Fountains

eldest surviving male of the Ottoman dynasty, but often the successor had spent so long in indulged isolation that he was unfit to rule.

Afternoon Tea

Return to the First Court and hail a taxi (always checking that the meter is on) for your next destination, the **Green Mansion**, (Yeşil Ev), at the eastern end of Sultanahmet Park behind the Haseki Sultan Hamamı. This 19th-century mansion, now converted to a hotel, is a great stop for late afternoon tea in the garden. To one side of the hotel is a *türbe*, or tomb, of an old Muslim saint; to the other is the 18th-century **Medrese of Cedid Mehmet Efendi** – now the **Istanbul Arts Bazaar**.

After a rest, walk to the **Arasta Bazaar**, a small, quiet street of carpet and collectors' shops with a particularly interesting selection of antique and Central Asian fabrics. These shops were originally built as part of the Blue Mosque complex to attract rent revenue. At the end of the street is the **Mosaic Museum** (9am–4.30pm, closed Tue; entrance fee) which is entered just behind the bazaar. The walkway once connected the emperor's palace (which was on the site of the Blue Mosque) to the Harbour of Bucoleon below. The museum is now all that remains of the Great Palace of gold trees and mechanical birds, showing part of an exquisite mosaic floor depicting mythological and hunting scenes. It is thought to have been commissioned by Justinian in the 6th century, and to have led from the royal apartments to the residential Palace of Daphne and the *kathisma*, the imperial box at the ancient Hippodrome.

After touring the Arasta Bazaar and museum, walk down the hill 270 metres (300yds) to the **Küçük Aya Sofya Camii** (closed for restoration), a former Byzantine church transformed into a mosque. Built by Justinian and Theodora in 527 as the **Church of Saints Sergius and Bacchus**, it is a tiny replica of Aya Sofya. The mosaics are no longer in place, but the dark green and red marble columns and carved frieze are originals.

About 50 metres (55yds) uphill to the north is the **Sokullu Mehmet Paşa Camii**, a mosque built by Mimar Sinan in 1571 for Esma Sultan, the daughter of Selim the Sot and wife of Sokullu Mehmet Paşa, a highly regarded Bosnian-born grand vizier who was assassinated in 1579. The mosque has some of Turkey's finest 16th-century Iznik tiles, and their unusual tulip motifs

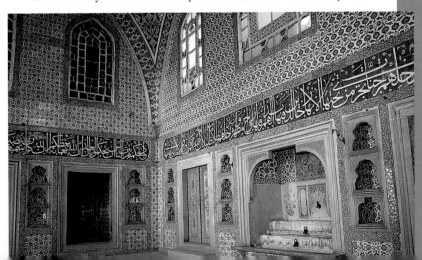

go up to the pendentives supporting the dome. Sokullu's mansion, just up-hill, has been restored and is now operated as the **Sokullu Paşa Hotel** (Mehmetpaşa Sokak 10, Sultanahmet), one of the most charming hotels in this district.

Kumkapı District

From the hotel, follow **Kadırga Liman Caddesi** to the district of **Kumkapı**, about 1km (½ mile) away, past some of the older neighbourhoods of the city, with their old wooden houses. Set along the Sea of Marmara, and a fisherman's quarter since Byzantine times, Kumkapı is run down but full of charm, and its restaurants serve the best fish in town.

It is also the Armenian quarter. A vast majority of Turkey's 70,000 Armenians are Gregorians who trace their conversion to Christianity to the

year 301, a generation before Constantine the Great adopted it as the state religion of the Roman Empire. Spend half an hour or so touring the historical sites nearby before returning for dinner.

Visit the **Armenian Patriarchate** in Şarapnel Sokak (Shrapnel Street), located off Kumkapı's main thoroughfare and Kadırga Liman Caddesi, several blocks to the west of Kumkapı Square. The Armenian Patriarch of Istanbul is subordinate to the Catholicos (Primate of the Armenian Church) at Echmiadzin, near Yerevan in Armenia. Across from the dilapidated building is the Patriarchate **Church of the Virgin Mary**, built in 1828, the principal Armenian shrine in the city. Several Armenian Patriarchs are buried on its premises, and it is open to the public.

The restaurants of Kumkapı are of the *meyhane* type, serving fish with an array of *meze* appetisers and *raki*, the national alcoholic beverage known as 'lion's milk'. Patrons are generally local Turks, intellectuals, journalists and foreigners. Several restaurants are Armenian-owned, including the **Kör Agop** (Blind Agop, ördekli Bakkal Sokak No 7), one of the most venerated establishments in the district. It specialises in *karides güveç*, a shrimp and cheese casserole, and *kırlangıç*, a tasty broiled tub fish in a frothy lemon base.

Another good eatery is **Fırat Restaurant** (Çakaktas Sok 11/A), which serves delightful *kalamar*, or fried squid. The **Üçler Balik Restaurant**, operated by an Albanian Turk, is also one of the best. Try some *pavurya*, crab meat served as a *meze*. Evenings can get crowded and boisterous. Gypsy musicians will often go from table to table, playing boisterous tunes for tips, while female performers sing sad songs of old Istanbul. Be generous, but watch your handbag and wallet, as the combination of alcohol and crowds generally make good pickings for thieves.

Above: fellow spirits in a bar in Kumkapı

3. ALONG THE BOSPHORUS *(see map, page 44)*

Enjoy a ferry ride through one of the world's most coveted waterways and see its splendid mansions; take a walk up the Anadolu Kavağı Fortress to view the Clashing Rocks and Black Sea; have a fish lunch; visit the sultans' many palaces and take a stroll through Yıldız Park.

The **Bosphorus** is not only beautiful, it is also one of the most strategically placed necks of water on earth, to which the intensity of ship traffic attests. Day three will be spent touring 'The Throat' by ferry and car.

Special tour boats leave three times a day in summer from the **Bosphorus Ferry Boat Landing** (Boğaz Vapurları Iskelesi) in Eminönü, a short walk northeast of the Galata Bridge. The two-way trip on the public ferry costs about US$7, and can get full in the summer, but it is nonetheless an enjoyable journey and a good way to rest your feet and escape the heat, crowds, cars and hustlers. The first boat doesn't leave until 10.30am, so there's time for some shopping around the Sirkeci and Eminönü business districts and street bazaars, or to take a walk along the Galata Bridge for a harbour view.

Alight at the last village, Anadolu Kavağı, for lunch. Sit out on deck to get the best view of the city, and in particular its 19th-century palaces and spectacular Bosphorus mansions *(yalisi)* – some old and crumbling; some vibrant, showy and new. There is plenty to look at: the Bosphorus is one of the busiest waterways in the world.

Between Europe and Asia

A narrow, twisting neck of water that severs Europe and Asia and connects the Black Sea with the Sea of Marmara, the Bosphorus is 30km (19 miles) in length, ballooning from a waist of 760 metres (830yds) to 3km (2 miles). A number of former towns, villages and tiny settlements cling to its scenic shores, which are still lined with plane trees and old wooden houses.

The Bosphorus gets its name from the mythical affair that Zeus, chief god of the Olympic pantheon, was having with the moon goddess Io. (In Turkish *ay*, pronounced 'eye', means moon). According to legend, Zeus's jealous wife, Hera, sent a swarm of gnats to irritate Io. The goddess then turned herself into a heifer, plunged into the waterway from the Asian shore, and swam across to escape the gnats. Thus the waterway was called the Bosphorus or 'Ford of the Cow'. The next mytho-historical event associated with the Bosphorus was the passage of the rebel Jason and his Argonauts on their way to seek the recovery of the Golden Fleece from the land of the Colchis, at the eastern end of the Black Sea, in about 1000BC. The passage has always been dangerous to shipping because of its erratic and deadly

Right: ferries on the Bosphorus

currents. The predominant surface current runs from the Black Sea to the Sea of Marmara, and a stronger subsurface current runs at a depth of 40 metres (145ft) in the opposite direction. Ancient mariners using only oars and sails used a sea anchor or fish net to catch the lower current when travelling up the Bosphorus to the Black Sea. Hundreds of giant supertankers and cargo ships pass through it daily, their numbers ever increasing due to the exportation of Russian, Central Asian and Caucasian oil. There is also a host of smaller craft: commuter ferry boats plying between the two banks, little coasters and fishing boats that zip and bob among the behemoths.

In addition to the danger presented by the unpredictable currents, thick fog descends without warning in winter, reducing visibility to zero. This problem is exacerbated by the effects of pollution.

The Bosphorus has always been coveted by the Black Sea nations, particularly by Tsarist Russia and the former Soviet Union, because it is that country's only outlet to the warm waters of the Mediterranean. By controlling the passage, the Turks, in the words of Winston Churchill, 'pinch Russia's nostrils'

Eyes to the Shore

Once the boat leaves dock, you quickly pass **Saray Burnu** with **Topkapı Palace** on your right. To your left is **Karaköy** and the main port facilities, with scores of giant Greek, Russian and European ocean liners shouldered to the pier. Almost next to the cruise terminal, in an old customs warehouse, is is Turkey's equivalent of the Guggenheim or Tate Modern, **Istanbul Modern** (Meclis-I Mebusan Caddesi Liman Sahası, Karaköy, tel: (0212) 3347300, www.istanbulmodern.org; open Tue–Sun 10am–6pm, Thur 10am–8pm and free until 2pm). A beau-

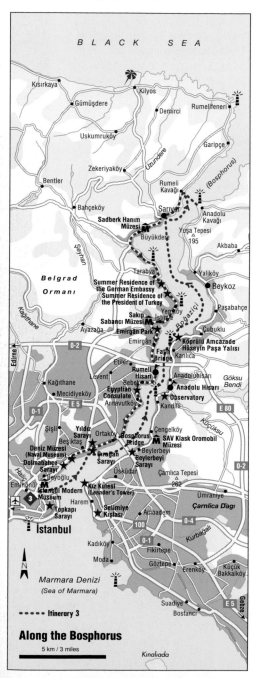

Along the Bosphorus

5 km / 3 miles

tifully converted modern art gallery, it has installations, video, photography, and touring exhibitions as well as painting and sculpture.

You can see the silhouettes of Istanbul's biggest hotels, the **Swissôtel**, the **Etap Marmara** and the **Hilton** in the hills, and a little further on, the twin towers of Sabancı Plaza. To your right is the Sea of Marmara and the start of the Asian shore of Istanbul. During the next three days of excursions, you will come back and visit many of the sites you pass by boat today.

Your boat soon glides by **Leander's Tower** (Kız Kulesi, tel: (021) 342 4747; tower open for visits noon–7pm; restaurant open to 1am), a lighthouse built as a defensive watch tower by Athenian statesman Alcibiades. It was reconstructed as a lighthouse in the 12th century by the Byzantine Emperor Manuel I Comnenus and dedicated to the legendary Leander, who drowned while swimming across to his loved one, the Priestess Hero. Now a restaurant, the lighthouse marks the beginning of the Bosphorus. To your left is **Mimar Sinan University**, a fine-arts college named after the 16th-century Turkish architect, and the lavishly ornate **Dolmabahçe Palace** (*see page 62*), the 19th-century home of the sultans in the twilight of empire. Behind it is İnönü Stadium, named after Turkey's second president, İsmet İnönü, where football matches and international rock concerts are held.

The Asian shore, to your right, is often neglected by visitors, but has a wealth of fascination and is easily reached by one of the swarm of small ferries from Eminönü. **Üsküdar** is one of the city's more conservative districts with numerous mosques including Sinan's **Atik Valide Sultan Camii**, the **Çinili Camii** (Tiled Mosque), the

Top: Ortaköy Mosque
Right: Leander's Tower

Semsi Paşa Camii and the **Yeni Valide Sultan Camii**. Other sights here include the vast **Selimiye Barracks**, one corner of which commemorates Florence Nightingale (to visit, fax: (0216) 5531009 two days in advance). It was here, during the Crimean War, that the lady with the lamp set up her Scutari hospital and founded modern nursing. The British Crimean cemetery and the vast **Karaca Ahmet Cemetery** are also worth a visit. Haydarpaşa Station is Istanbul's main rail link with Asia; tunnels to connect both train and metro under the Bosphorus have been held up by archaeological finds.

Istanbul Oyuncak Muzesi (Ömerpaşa Caddesi, Dr. Zeki Zeren Sokagi 17, Göztepe, tel: (0216) 3594550/1; open 9.30am–6pm Tue–Fri; till 7pm Sat–Sun) is an utterly charming toy museum, one man's labour of love that enchants adults and children. Büyük **Çamlica (Big Pine Hill)** is the highest point in Istanbul, an open hill with fabulous views and space to run around and blow away the cobwebs.

Just to the south of Üsküdar is **Kadıköy**, the ancient Greek town of Chalcedon and the oldest settlement in the region, founded in 675BC. It's a wonderful place to stroll, with a huge flea market on Tuesdays and a nostalgic tram that runs down to trendy **Moda**; here, Bagdat Caddesiş is one of the best shopping and entertainment districts in the city.

Back on the European shore, the boat soon stops at **Beşiktaş**, one of Istanbul's most populous districts, to take on more passengers. Note the **Naval Museum** (Deniz Müzesi), which is full of splendid Ottoman caiques *(see page 52)*. From here the boat passes the splendidly restored **Çırağan Palace**, which has become the plush Kempinski Hotel on the European side and is a good venue for afternoon tea or cocktails. Before it burned down in 1910, this had been the site of the Parliament Building for the two years following the 1908 revolution of the Young Turks. Behind it, up the hill, is Yıldız Park, which you will visit on the return journey.

Islands and Palaces

Ortaköy, or Middle Village – so-called because it is supposedly at the midway mark of the Bosphorus – has a fine 19th-century mosque standing next to the **Bosphorus Bridge**. Built in 1973, this is the fifth-longest suspension

bridge in the world and the second-longest in Istanbul. On the Asian side, you can see the **Beylerbeyi Palace** (Çayırbaflı Caddesi, tel: (0216) 3219320; open Tue, Wed, Fri–Sun 9am–5pm, to 4pm Oct–Apr), by the bridge's huge pier. This lovely palace, which holds chamber music concerts during the June Istanbul Music Festival, was constructed in 1865 by Sarkis Balyan, a member of a 19th-century Armenian family of architects. It served as a summer lodge for foreign dignitaries and was an escape for Sultan Abdülaziz from his brother's overwhelming Dolmabahçe.

Next you pass **Galatasaray Adası**, a tiny island owned by the Galatasaray sports club. A favourite summer hang-out for Istanbul businessmen, it has a swimming pool, a restaurant and games rooms. To your right is **Çengelköy**, the Village of Hooks, so-called because after the Turkish conquest anchor hooks were discovered there. **Sadullah Paşa Yalısı**, the dark red 19th-century mansion, takes its name from an Ottoman diplomat called Sadullah Paşa, who was one of its owners. The **SAV Klasik Otomobil Müzesi** (104 Natoyolu Bosna Bulvarı, Çengelköy; tel: (0216) 3295030; closed Mon) is a private collection of over 100 gorgeous vintage cars including Ferraris and Lamborghinis. Nearby is **Kuleli Kışlası**, a military barracks with towers built in 1828, now serving as the Military High School.

Bosphorus Villages

The next village that you will pass on your left is **Arnavutköy**, or the Albanian Village, which has numerous Orthodox churches and pleasant seafood restaurants. The waterfront here is lined by a particularly elaborate collection of *yalıs*, the 19th-century wooden mansions with gingerbread trim that were popular amongst the aristocracy who followed the court's move from the Topkapı down to the Dolmabahçe. Many were close to total dereliction before recent renovation. One street back from the sea front, there are still plenty looking for salvation. On a hill overlooking the town is **Robert College**, an American co-educational high school established by US missionaries in 1871 as the **American College for Girls**. It is the most sought-after private school in the country and the *alma mater* of many Turkish politicians.

Turning at the hook known as **Akıntı Burnu** (Cape of Currents), the deepest part of the Bosphorus, one comes to **Bebek**, a fashionable district where wealthy businessmen, glamorous movie stars and foreign dignitaries reside. On the hill stands the buildings of **Bosphorus University**, established in 1971 on the grounds of old Robert College. If you look to the Asian side, you will see the township of **Kandilli**, famed for the **Kandilli Observatory**, established in 1911. You can also see the **Count Ostorog Yalısı**, a seaside mansion built by a French nobleman of Polish descent who served in a high position in the Ottoman court in the early 1900s. The Beykoz area was an Ottoman Imperial playground, with picnic parties rowing across

Left: Küçüksu Palace
Above: gliding along the Bosphorus

to the river outlet they named the 'Sweet Waters of Asia'. The **Küçüksu Kasrı** (Küçüksu Caddesi, Beykoz, tel: (0216) 3323303; 9.30am–4pm, closed Mon, Thur) was built as a hunting lodge for Sultan Abdul Mecit in 1857 by Nikogos Balyan, of the illustrious Armenian family of architects. Elaborately decorated with stucco, crystal and carpets, it has been used for state entertaining. Nearby is the **Kıbrıslı Mustafa Emin Paşa Yalısı**, built in 1760, the largest wooden mansion on the Bosphorus with a façade 60 metres (66 yds) long.

The boat now zips past the two castles known as the 'Cut Throats' (Boğaz Kesen), **Rumeli Hisarı** (*see page 51*) on the European side and the smaller **Anadolu Hisarı** on the Asian side of the straits. Built by the Turks before the conquest, they were intended to strangle any aid to the besieged city from the Black Sea. The fortresses stand at the narrowest point of the waterway, and it was here that the Persian King Darius built a bridge of boats in 512BC to transport his huge army in a campaign against the Scythians.

You next pass **Fatih Bridge**, the third-longest suspension bridge in the world. Built in 1987 by a Japanese-Turkish consortium, it is named after Fatih Sultan Mehmet (Mehmet II), the conqueror of Istanbul.

The boat then stops off at **Kanlıca**, a picturesque village on the Asian shore with quaint seaside fish restaurants and coffeehouses, known for its creamy yogurt served with a heaped spoon of sugar. On the European side you can see the village of **Emirgân**, famous for its immense park with tulip gardens and home to the fabulous Sakıp Sabancı Museum (*see page 50*).

Fish Restaurants Galore

The Bosphorus veers sharply to the left after **Tarabya** and enters **Büyükdere Koyu**, the Bay of Büyükdere, where it widens to 3km (2 miles). The boat stops at **Sarıyer**, a large township on the European shore, then proceeds to **Rumeli Kavağı**, a pleasant fisherman's village with fishing boats tied up at the wharf. The mouth of the Black Sea can be seen from here.

Above: selling the day's catch

The boat then crosses to Asia and comes to its last halt, **Anadolu Kavağı**, where it will remain for two or three hours. This will give you the opportunity to have lunch and explore the village, famed for its fish restaurants that serve meals to suit all tastes and pockets. Go for a grilled mackerel sandwich, eaten on a bench under a plane tree, or for a sumptuous sit down meal of fried *kalkan* (turbot) or grilled *lüfer* (blue fish), with appetisers such as *midye tava* (fried mussels), *zeytinyağlı barbunya* (beans served in olive oil), and *haydari*, a delicious yogurt dip mixed with garlic and parsley, served at any of the restaurants. The best times to eat fish are late summer and autumn.

The Clashing Rocks

Anadolu Kavağı, you will soon see, is a military zone. After lunch, walk to the **Genoese Fortress** on top of the hill. From this vantage point there is a sweeping view of the upper reaches of the Bosphorus and the entrance to the Black Sea. The rocky formations on either side of the Bosphorus near the mouth of the Black Sea were known in ancient times as the **Symplegades**,

or Clashing Rocks, because it was widely believed they slammed together to crush ships trying to pass through the straits. These Clashing Rocks were one of the many trials that Jason and the Argonauts had to deal with in their search for the Golden Fleece.

Return to your boat, which should be leaving for Istanbul, but get off at the next stop, **Rumeli Kavağı**, across the Bosphorus, and hire a taxi for the afternoon. Drive back to Istanbul along the European shore, visiting many of the sites you saw from the boat. On a hill halfway between Rumeli Kavağı and the town of Sarıyer is the **Tomb of Telli Baba** a Muslim saint. It is a firm belief among traditional Turkish families that a visit to the tomb and a prayer to the saint helps unmarried women find husbands. After their weddings, it is common for brides to come and tie bits of cloth, silver wire and talismanic coils by the tree in front of the tomb as a mark of gratitude.

Sarıyer is known for its colourful fish market and seafood restaurants. Aquarius 1 and the Deniz Kızı (Mermaid) both serve an array of tantalising appetisers with their main fish courses. Both are located in the local fish bazaar. Another recommendation is Sarıyer Muhallebicisi, a pudding shop in the main street, which has the reputation of serving the best desserts in Istanbul, including *tavuk göğüsü*, made from pigeon breast.

Sadberk Hanım Museum (Büyükdere Caddesi 27–29; 10am–5pm, closed

Above: a typical fish restaurant along the upper Bosphorus

Wed; entrance fee), one of Turkey's few private museums, is the highlight of the next township, **Büyükdere**, and is worth a half-hour's visit. Located in an old Greek *yalı*, it is run by a foundation established by Vehbi Koç, one of Turkey's leading industrialists. It includes antiquities dating from 6,000BC to the fall of Constantinople in 1453. It also has a good collection of Turkish ethnographic objects and a display showing life in a 19th-century Bosphorus seaside mansion.

A row of 19th-century foreign embassy summer residences, including the German, French, British, Russian, Austrian and Italian, line the Bosphorus near the village of **Tarabya**. The garden of the **Summer Residence of the German Embassy** can be entered with the doorkeeper's permission. It contains the tombs of thousands of German soldiers killed in Russia during World War II. Nearby are the Summer Residence of the President of Turkey and Kalender Ordu Evi, a magnificent officers' club.

The next communities on your route are **Yeniköy**, a splendid high-society suburb, and **Istinye**, a tiny bay village – although it is not likely to stay that way for much longer, as the thriving **Istanbul Stock Exchange** has opened just above it. *The Savarona*, a magnificently renovated yacht which once belonged to Kemal Atatürk, is usually docked by the quayside in Istinye.

Emirgân's Tulip Park

In the next town, **Emirgân**, take a quick tour of the delightful **Emirgân Park**, renovated and operated by the Automobile and Touring Association. It has three pavilions, the **Pink Kiosk**, the **Yellow Chalet**, where refreshments are served, and the **White Pavilion**, where classical music performances are given. The park was owned by the Khedives of Egypt (title given to the Turkish viceroys of Egypt 1867–1914) who built the pavilions.

The best time to visit Emirgân is in spring, when red, yellow and blue tulips blanket the park, and the annual tulip festival takes place. Tulip growing originated in the private parks along the Bosphorus among Ottoman notables of the early 18th century – growing and trading the plant, native to Turkey, had been a craze that threatened to crash economies in western Europe.

Emirgân also has the **Sakıp Sabancı Museum** (Istinye Caddesi, tel: (0212) 2772200; open Tue–Sun 10am–6pm, Wed 10am–10pm), in the former home of one of Turkey's leading industrial families. The Atli Kösk (Horse Mansion) is named after the sculpted horse in the lush gardens. It is filled with family furniture, memorabilia and Turkish art and calligraphy. Onto this have been added a chic café/restaurant and an art gallery that houses major inter-

Above: castle at Rumeli Hisarı
Right: relaxing at Ortaköy

national touring exhibitions.There are several peaceful coffee houses on the village square beneath plane trees facing the Bosphorus.

Balta Limanı, the next town, is famous for the Büyük Reşit Paşa Yalısı, a 19th-century mansion now used as the Balta Liman Orthopedics Hospital. The enclosed area immediately behind the hospital is the **Mansion of Damat Mehmet Ferit Paşa** (1853–1923), one of the last grand viziers of the Ottoman Empire. The mansion and its surrounding buildings together serve as the Social Centre of Istanbul University.

Rumeli Castle

When you reach the town of **Rumeli Hisarı**, visit the enormous fortification of the same name (9am–4.30pm, closed Wed) that dominates the European shore of the Bosphorus. It was constructed by Mehmet II in 1452, one year before his conquest of Constantinople. The castle is 250 metres (273yds) in length and 125 metres (137yds) at its broadest point. Spanning a deep valley, it has two tall towers on the opposite hills and one at the bottom of the valley by the shoreline. During the Istanbul Festivals, it is used to stage plays, including Shakespeare's *Hamlet*, *Macbeth* and *Othello*.

Return to your taxi and drive to Bebek and Arnavutköy. The large grey 19th-century building on your left is the **Egyptian Consulate**. Arnavutköy has many old wooden houses; some are in ruins but those that have been saved and restored are now worth a small fortune. Half a dozen Orthodox churches, include the impressive **Ayi Strati Araksiarhi** near the post office.

Continuing from Arnavutköy, you will pass through the villages of **Kuruçeşme**, which has many outstanding restaurants, and **Ortaköy**, which has a popular flea market and crafts fair on Sundays as well as many trendy, upmarket cafés and nightspots. Reach the enchanting **Yıldız Park** (open daily 9am–6pm, 5.30pm in winter), the biggest public park in Istanbul, for late afternoon tea. Have your taxi driver take you to the very top so you can tour its two pavilions and two *serras*, or winter coffeehouses.

The park was part of **Yıldız Palace**, a latter-day residence of the Ottoman sultans that lies just northwest of the grounds. At Yıldız, you can admire

the creations of the tragic Abdülhamid II, the last of the great sultans who became, amid the self-imposed solitude of his palace, one of the most accomplished carpenters of his empire. The **Palace Museum** (Yildiz Caddesi, tel: (0212) 2583377; 9.30am–4.30pm; entrance fee) is filled with the Sultan's superb collection of porcelain. Take time also to appreciate the perfectly reproduced Viennese and Swiss cafés in the vast park surrounding the palace, which once served him (their only customer). In the 1980s the park and buildings were restored by the Turkish Touring and Automobile Association; in 1995 control of the park reverted to the city authorities, who have been accused of letting standards slip. The brick-red **Çadır** (Tent) **Pavilion**, which overlooks a large pool of goldfish, was the site where Ahmet Sefik Mithat Paşa (1822–84), the grand vizier responsible for preparing the Ottoman Empire's first constitution in 1878 and establishing the first National Assembly, was tried on trumped-up charges of murdering Abdül Aziz (sultan 1861–76). Found guilty, he was exiled to Yemen and executed.

Tea in Yıldız Park

Resembling a pink mushroom, the **Pink Serra**, or Winter Garden, serves as a fancy pastry shop in winter. Everything inside the building is pink and white. The floor is pink marble, while the antique plates and decanters displayed in glass cases are wine-coloured. The **Green Serra**, another patisserie, is located under high trees in a valley just beyond the Pink Serra. The Green Serra's winter garden is decked with green tables, chairs and lanterns that harmonise with the surroundings. During the reign of Sultan Abdülhamit, the **Malta Kiosk** was used to host official receptions. The Kiosk has a pleasant courtyard framed by blossoming Judas trees and bougainvillaea.

After visiting Yıldız Park return to the main avenue running along the Bosphorus and drop by the Cirağan Palace, now converted into a world class hotel, restaurant and convention centre. The interior has been delightfully restored using pastel colours and crystal bannisters. In the next town along the route, Beşiktaş, visit the **Mausoleum of Barbarossa Hayrettin**, the Ottoman grand admiral whose navies turned the Mediterranean into a Turkish lake in the 16th century. In the park just behind the mausoleum you can see the **Statue of Barbarossa Hayrettin**. Lines written by the poet Yahya Kemal Beyatlı (1884–1958) are inscribed on the southern side of the pedestal:

> *Whence on the sea's horizons comes that roar?*
> *Can it be Barbarossa now returning*
> *From Tunis or Algiers or from the Isles?*
> *Two hundred vessels ride upon the waves.*
> *Coming from lands the rising Crescent lights:*
> *O blessed ships, from what seas are ye come?*

If the two-storey **Naval Museum** (Deniz Müzesi; 9am–5pm, Wed–Sun; entrance fee), located behind the statue, is still open when you get there, be sure to visit it. The museum has a good collection of artefacts from various

Left: the new Turkey

naval engagements fought by the Turks over the centuries. These include battles against the Venetians in the 16th century, the Dardanelles campaign of 1915 against the British and French, and the 1974 Cyprus conflict fought against the Greeks and Greek Cypriots.

Its garden is littered with naval artillery, as well as the anchors and propellers of famous Turkish warships. A mural map of the Ottoman Empire at its zenith is displayed on its wall. In the garden is the wreck of a German U-boat that hit a mine and sank off the Black Sea mouth of the Bosphorus during World War I. The wreckage of the submarine was discovered in 1993 by miners digging for coal in an area that had been reclaimed from the sea. Another part of the museum, which faces the Hayrettin Iskelesi, or Hayrettin Boat Landing, displays the **Sultans' Galleys** (*Padisah Kayıkları*), which the sultans used for outings with their harems.

After-dark Dining

When you have finished sightseeing, dinner options include the chic international restaurant, **Hünal's Brasserie**, which occupies one of the beautiful restored houses of Akaretler Sıraevleri (above the North Shield Pub) or the Ottoman Tuğra Restaurant, overlooking the Bosphorus at the Ciragan Palace, where superb food is accompanied by live Fasil music. In keeping with the area's swanky reputation, these restaurants require advance booking and there is a smart dress code.

If you prefer a more down-to-earth evening in Istanbul, head to the Taksim/Beyoğlu district where you can choose from colourful *meyhanes* such as those in Nevizade Sok or **Çiçek Pasajı** in Istiklâl Caddesi's bustling fish bazaar. Gypsy music is pretty much guaranteed at all of these places. In this area, hotels such as the Four Seasons offer pricier fine-dining. Another option – if you arrive early in the evening – is the re-opened **Pano's Historic Greek Wine Bar** (Tarihi Pano Şarapahanesi) at the corner of Meşrutiyet Caddesi, which is popular with the young foreign community. The restaurant serves cheap wine by the bottle and very good food.

Above: dervishes whirl in an ecstatic trance in the Yıldız Palace ballroom

4. A TOUR OF THE NEW CITY *(see map, page 55)*

Visit the 'far side' of old European Istanbul; see the sights from the 14th-century Galata Tower; take an architectural stroll through through the city's old passages and artist's quarter; treat yourself to an invigorating rub-down at a Turkish baths and join a tour of the magnificent Dolmabahçe Palace.

Though referred to as 'the New City', the district of **Karaköy**, Beyoğlu and Taksim Square isn't really new at all, but was, and still is, the district favoured by foreign residents, and for this reason has traditionally been home to the non-Muslim pastimes of taverns and ribald entertainment. Even to-

day Beyoğlu is the city's 'fun' quarter, and is full of nightclubs, bars, cinemas, theatres, bistros and patisseries.

It was first known as Galata, after the Celts (or Gauls) who besieged the city during Roman times, but then stayed on to enjoy it, and later Pera, which in Greek meant 'the far side', being 'beyond' the Old City (Stamboul) across the Golden Horn. To the Muslim Ottoman Turks it was simply Giâvurşehiri, the City of the Infidel, because it was almost entirely inhabited by Christian Greeks, Armenians, Venetians, Genoese, British and Jews, international traders who lived in splendid stone mansions, many of which can be seen today.

In its 19th-century heyday, the languages spoken in Pera were mainly French, Italian and Greek, and there were hundreds of high-class dance halls, tavernas, cabarets and theatres where European entertainers performed and alcohol flowed freely. It was a part of the city avoided and shunned by the pious Turks, who looked disapprovingly upon its nightlife, but greatly appreciated by others, who could acclimatise themselves to western practice without leaving home. The western-minded founder of the Turkish Republic, Kemal Atatürk, was one such enthusiast. Sumptuous embassy buildings, which were downgraded to consulates after the Turkish capital was moved to Ankara in 1923, still line **Istiklâl Caddesi** (the Grand Rue de Pera), today pedestrianised and a major shopping thoroughfare. Wealthy Christian inhabitants have all but disappeared, to be replaced by Turkish peasant migrants, but these in turn are slowly being displaced by young, educated Turks and foreign residents in a trend towards urban renewal.

The district acquired its present form under the Genoese. After the Byzantine Emperors reconquered Constantinople from the Latins in 1261,

Above: view from the Galata Bridge
Right: in the picture outside Faience Mosque

the area around Galata Tower was declared a semi-autonomous Genoese colony, ruled by a *podesta*, or governor, appointed by Genoa. The Genoese fortified their town, constructing protective walls around it, and built the famous watchtower at its centre. After the conquest, the Turks removed the walls, but the district remained the European quarter of Constantinople. Old engravings of the neighbourhood, available in most gift shops, illustrate how it once appeared.

Most of the religious edifices in the district are Christian churches, many of them still in use, but there are also a number of synagogues, which serve a diminishing Jewish population. In 1900 their population totalled 300,000, most of whom were of Sephardic origin, but today it has dwindled to about 25,000. Mosques were primarily built along the shore on land reclaimed from the Bosphorus. Many were erected in the 19th century in baroque and rococo styles, displaying the preferences of their Christian architects and the strong influence of the West on late Islamic art.

Mosque of the Moors

Begin your tour of Karaköy at **Arap Camii**, Kalyon Sok 1, on a side street just off **Tersane Caddesi** (Shipyards Street) around 9am. This mosque, originally the 14th-century church of SS Paul and Dominic, was named after Moorish refugees who joined the flight of Jews from Spain in 1492. The square belfry makes a rather unconventional minaret, with the cross at the

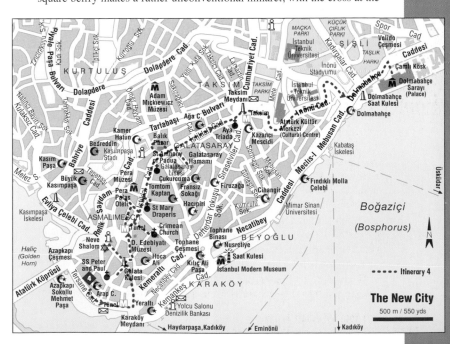

top now a Islamic crescent. The Turks also added the ablutions fountain. Walk to Tersane Caddesi and turn north in the direction of the Bosphorus. This area, **Perşembe Pazarı**, or the Thursday Bazaar, is the principal market for hardware. You then pass the **Tünel**, a two-stop, 550-metre (1,800-ft) metro built by the French in 1874 to connect Karaköy and Beyoğlu.

You now enter **Karaköy Square**, a busy intersection. Vendors on the underground passages ahead sell electrical goods at cut-rate prices. To your right is the Galata Bridge and the Golden Horn and to your left is **Yüksek Kaldırım**, or 'High Steps', a steep, paved street that leads to the Galata Tower. The building with a tower-like crown standing at the corner of Yüksek Kaldırım and **Bankalar Caddesi** (Avenue of the Banks) was the ancient **Podestat**, the **Palace of the Genoese Governor of Pera**. Straight ahead of you a road leads round past the famous Gülluoğlu Baklava shop to Istanbul Modern and the Bosphorus shore.

If you don't want to trek uphill, return to the Tünel tram and walk back down hill from the Istiklâl stop to Galata Tower, which has a shady, inexpensive and congenial teahouse at the bottom. Karaköy is said to derive its name from the Karaite Jewish sect who once lived here; a number of old and disused Jewish religious buildings are to the left along Bankalar Caddesi.

Jewish History

The first restored mansion you see, immediately on your left along the stairway, belonged to the Camondo family of bankers, and is now a hotel. Count Albert Camondo was born in Ortaköy, and helped found the first Jewish school, but ran into trouble with the city's more conservative rabbis for daring to include Turkish and French lessons in the curriculum. On the street parallel, to your right, is a large **Aşkenazi** synagogue. Modern **Neve Shalom**, at Büyük Hendek Street, immediately to the west of Galata Tower, serves the needs of most of Istanbul's Jewish community today. In November 2003 it was the target, along with the Beth Israel Synagogue, of a massive Al Qaeda bomb, which left 25 dead and 300 injured.

Passing old houses and a few antique shops, you can't miss the the **Galata Tower** (daily 9am–8pm; entrance fee) built by Genoese settlers in 1348 to defend their colony. It is on the site of an earlier wooden tower erected in 507

by Byzantine Emperor Anastasius I. The 12-storey tower is 61 metres (200ft) high. In the early 17th century, a Turkish daredevil, Hezarfen Ahmet Şelebi, supposedly jumped from the tower in an early version of a hangglider and flew across the Bosphorus. Unfortunately the clergy and sultans took offence at this escapade and he was later executed. His memory lives on in Turkish film and folklore as a celebration of freedom and the flaunting of authority. There is a copper illustration of Şelebi's flight

Left: a quiet smoke at Galata Bridge

on the wall to the right of the ground-floor elevator. Take this elevator to the top for a sweeping view of the city, including the Golden Horn, the Galata and Atatürk bridges, Topkapı Palace, Aya Sofya, the Blue Mosque, the Bosphorus and the Sea of Marmara. There is a restaurant and nightclub at the top where a traditional floor show includes belly dancing.

SS Peter and Paul, a Dominican church attended mostly by Italian speakers, is on Galata Kulesi Sokak, on the left-hand descent from the Tower toward the sea. Originally from the 15th century, it was rebuilt by the Fossati brothers in 1853. Gravestones show evidence of the large Maltese community of Istanbul which adopted it in the mid-19th century. You will see many more European remnants on this street, including an Armenian house, later the British Jail under post-World War I Allied occupation.

Back to the tower, and up to your right, **Galip Dede Caddesi** is home to the **Librairie de Pera** (Galip Dede Caddesi No 22), one of the best places to look for historical books. You will also notice on the approach through İstiklâl Caddesi that the street is lined with music shops stocking everything from rock equipment to traditional instruments and CDs. Galip Dede Sokak gets its name from the **Mausoleum** (Türbe) **of Galip Dede**, a Mevlevi Dervish (member of a mystic Islamic religious order), on the right-hand side of the street.

Dervishes Museum

Through the gates is the former *tekke,* a monastery of the **Whirling Dervishes** (Sun and Mon 9.30am– 4.30pm; entrance fee). Dervish orders were banned in the early days of the Republic, and so officially this *tekke* is the **Divan Edebiyatı Müzesi**, a museum of classical Ottoman poetry and musical instruments. But a rather new-age group of Whirling Dervishes perform their ritual dance *(sema)* every second Sunday in summer, for a small donation. In this particular order, most of the members are young, and women participate in the ritual along-

Above: Dolmabahçe Palace from the Bosphorus
Right: ornamental vase in the grounds of the Palace

side men. The music accompanying the *sema* is hauntingly beautiful and CDs can be bought on the premises. Also on the grounds is the **Tomb of Kumbaracı** (Bombardier) **Ahmet Paşa**, the French officer Count Bonneval who joined the Ottoman Army umder Mahmut I (1730–54) and was named Commandant of the Artillery Corps. Bonneval converted to Islam, adopted a Turkish name and died in 1747. The cemetery of Ibrahim Müteferrika (1670–1745), who established the first printing press in the Ottoman Empire, is nearby.

Artist Quarter

You have now reached **Istiklâl Caddesi** (Avenue of Independence) and the terminal for the tram that runs to Taksim, collecting passengers from the *Tünel*. Across from the tram stop, the restored **Passage du Tünel** is one of many graceful turn-of-the-century shopping arcades in Pera. It specialises in art and antique shops, and there is an excellent coffee and cake shop, '1001', at the far end. At the back of the passage you enter Sofyali Sokak and Istanbul's artist quarter of **Asmalımescit**, a pedestrian-only network of streets where there are currently more than 40 artists' studios and a few small galleries along with teahouses and restaurants. There is an excellent contemporary jazz club, **Babylon**, on Şeybender, and at the corner of Minare Sokak, the Art Nouveau mansion of the sultan's stovemaker has been renovated to house a restaurant and cybercafé.

Left on Asmalımescit Sokak, just past the popular **Yakup II** restaurant, is the home of Donizetti Paşa, founder of the Ottoman Imperial Band (which replaced the traditional Jannisary mehter band), and elder brother of opera composer Gaetano Donizetti. But the most famous landmark of old Beyoğlu is the century-old hotel made famous by Agatha Christie, the **Pera Palas** (www.perapalas.com; closed for renovation until late 2008), which has its

original 19th-century furniture and fittings. Built to serve the needs of those travelling on the **Orient Express** from Paris, it had a reputation for intrigue. Of the spies who lurked in its corridors, the most famous was Mata Hari, but famous figures from Trotsky to Marilyn Monroe have stayed here.

Across the road the former Hotel Bristol has been converted into the **Pera Museum** (Meşrutiyet Caddesi 141, Tepebaşı ; tel:(0212) 3349900; open Tue–Sat 10am–7pm, Sun noon–6pm), which has a curious but attractive combination of Ottoman paintings and Anatolian weights and measures, along with a posh coffee shop and jazz concerts.

Reminders of Swinging Pera

Back on Istiklâl, circle back to Tünel to get a picture of the grand embassy buildings and art nouveau houses from the days of swinging Pera *(see page 54)*. First on your right is the late 17th-century **Swedish Embassy**. Common enmity toward Russia made the Swedes (and the Poles) important allies of the Ottoman Empire. Next to it is the lavish Art Nouveau **Botter House**, and a right turn on Şahkulu Bostanı leads to the **Crimean Memorial Church** (Christ Church, open for services every Sunday) the largest Protestant church in Istanbul, on Serdar-i Ekrem Sokak. It was constructed in 1868 by Lord Stratford de Redcliffe, designed by G.E. Street, architect of the London Law Courts, and named after the British soldiers who died in the Crimean War.

Returning to Istiklâl, the **Russian Embassy** is followed by a Catholic church, **St Mary Draperis**, built by Franciscans in 1789, and possibly the only Catholic church in the world with an inscription commemorating a Muslim Monarch, Abdülhamid. The old **French Consulate**, now the French Cultural Centre, off Postacılar Caddesi was used as a plague hospital in 1719. It is older than most of the other embassies, as France was the first European country befriended by the Ottomans. The present building was erected in 1831 after fire destroyed the original 16th-century palace, but the **Chapel of St Louis** dates to 1581, a pretty example of French Renaissance. Across the street the **Rejans** restaurant (Emir Nevruz Sokak) is tucked away in an alley. It was opened by aristocratic Russian refugees after World War I and serves delicious *borscht*, *piroshky*, Chicken Kievsky, and schnitzel with lemon vodka.

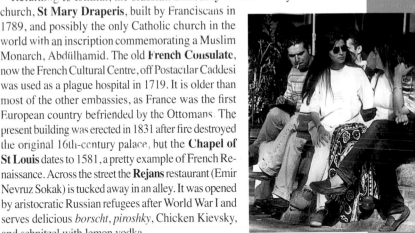

The **Dutch Embassy**, like the Russian, was built in the mid 19th century by the Swiss-Italian Fossati brothers, who also undertook the first great renovation of Aya Sofya in modern times. A Dutch Reform chapel, **Union Church**, is entered by a side street a short distance down hill on the right.

Around the corner from the Dutch Consulate is the popular **Garibaldi Restaurant and B ar** (Istiklâl Cad Odakule Yanı, Perukar Şıkmazı 1, Beyoğlu), near the site where Giuseppe Garibaldi (1807–82), the Italian patriot and revolutionary credited with the unification of the Italian state, lived in the 1830s while working as a captain of cargo ships sailing from the Mediterranean to the Black Sea. The building is owned by the Italian

Left: exterior and interior of Dolmabahçe Palace, with its famous chandelier
Above: taking time out

community, whose social club, **Societa Operaia Italiana**, on the top floor, is entered from the other end. Further up Istiklâl, to your left, the cobbled, 19th-century **Hacopulo Pasajı**, known locally as the 'button pasaj' for the cheap finery found there, leads to the **British Consulate** built in 1845 by Sir Charles Barry, architect of the Houses of Parliament in London. This architectural treat, was virtually demolished by an Al Qaeda bomb in November 2003, killing 14 people, including the Consul General.

The Catholic Church

Back across Istiklâl is the Franciscan **Church of St Anthony of Padua** (Sen Antuan), the largest Catholic shrine in Istanbul. Today fewer than 20,000 Catholics live in Turkey, almost all of them in Istanbul. A tiny chapel in the crypt serves the 200-strong community of Chaldean Christians, members of the ancient Nestorian Church now in union with Rome. Chaldean-rite Catholics in Turkey number about 5,000, most living in the mountains of the southeast. Services are held in either Arabic or Aramaic, the ancient language of Jesus. The Catholic churches of Istanbul also allow the Syrian Orthodox (who have no chapels in the city) to hold services at special hours.

A little further up Istiklâl you reach **Galatasaray Square**, named after **Galatasaray Lisesi**, the second-oldest institution of learning in the city after Istanbul University, visible on your right. Described by Turks as Mektebi Sultaniye, the **Sultan's School**, it was established in the late 15th century by Sultan Beyazıt II to train imperial pages, subordinate to the Palace School at Topkapı Sarayı. Galatasaray played an enormous role in Turkey's modernisation and westernisation in the 20th century, producing a great number of graduates who eventually became distinguished civil servants, politicians and diplomats. Behind the school is **Fransız Sokağı** (French

Street), a narrow alley that has been done up as a small corner of Istanbul that is forever Paris, with French restaurants, shops, cafés and even Parisian street-lamps.

The ornate building across from the high school on the western side of Istiklâl Caddesi is the **Cité de Pera**, built in 1876, a baroque structure lined with colourful outdoor bistros, tavernas, and restaurants that is usually called **Çiçek Pasajı**, or **Flower Sellers' Alley**. Once top hat and tails only, today it is one of the most popular tourist attractions and drinking spots in Istanbul. Note the caryatids (support columns modelled on the female form) above the entrance. Parallel to the passage is the famous **Balık Pazar** or Central Fish Market, a haven of gourmet shops

Left: Flower Sellers' Alley

selliing spices as well as fish and vegetables. On the right, halfway down the bazaar, is the easy-to-miss entrance to the **Üç Horan** Armenian church, its calm courtyard a stark contrast to the drinking dens around it. **Nevizade Sokak**, off to the right towards the back of the bazaar, is a wilder version of the Çiçek Pasaji, with seating outside. On summer weekends get there well before 8pm if you want a seat. Gypsy music is guaranteed as well as the presence of the indefatigable Madame Anahit, whose out-of-tune accordion can be silenced only with a tip. Fish is the main feature of the many restaurants surrounding (and inside) the bazaar, washed down with beer and *raki*, but it is also the place to try Armenian specialities such as *topik*, a *meze* of meat, raisins, cinnamon and other spices in a cake of broad bean paste. The **Boncuk Balikpazari** restaurant is recommended.

Wash and Brush-up

Return to Istiklâl Caddesi. Just to the left of Galatasaray Lisesi is a narrow alley leading to Turnacıbaşı Sokak. Note the charming Art Deco **Café Urban**, originally a Jewish pâtisserie, before reaching Turnacıbaşı, where a right turn leads to the **Galatasaray Hamamı**, (Turnacıba_ı Sokak 24, off

Iştiklal Caddesi; tel: (212) 2524242; 7am–10pm (men); 8am–8pm (women) daily), built for Sultan Beyazid II in 1481. This is one of the oldest and finest baths in Istanbul, and popular with local high society and tourists alike, although the men's section does have a reputation as a gay hangout.

Taking a bath at a *hamam* is for many people one of the highlights of a visit to Istanbul, and should not be missed, whether you decide to do it now, closer to Sultanahmet (which also has a number of historic bath houses) or at one of the city's five-star hotels. Most Turkish baths have three different temperature sections: a *camekân*, or reception chamber with dressing rooms around a cool court; the *soğukluk* or tepidarium, of middle temperature; and the *hararet*, or hot room, where one actually bathes. Leave at least two hours for the maximum *hamam* experience. Come hangover or hot weather you'll feel like a new penny when you emerge.

Antique hunters might like to follow Turnacıbaşı into the neighbourhood of **Çukurcuma**, left and right down the hill, where there are many junk shops and antique dealers. Otherwise, continuing up Istiklâl, this stretch is famous for its majestic passages, many of which have become cinema complexes with bars,

Above: Madam Anahit performs before patrons
Right: relaxing in a traditional Turkish bath

bistros, antique stores and CD shops. Look for the Alkazar at No 179, the Aleppo Passage at No 138, and the Emek Pasajı at No 124 which once housed the exclusive club Cercle d'Orient. The Cité Roumelie, at No 88, was built by Ragip Paşa, palace chamberlain, one of the small number of Turks who joined the European Pera crowd in its heyday.

Ağa Camii is the only functioning mosque in the immediate district, and dates from the 16th century. **Imam Adnan Sokak** (left) and **Büyükparmakkapı** (right) are both bursting with bars and clubs of all descriptions, and at **Meşelik Sokak** is the imposing late 19th-century Greek church, **Aya Triada**, the **Orthodox Church of the Holy Trinity** and the largest operational Greek church in Istanbul. It is overlooked by the popular **Hacı Baba** restaurant, another of tonight's options.

Taksim Square and Dolmabahçe Palace

You are now at **Taksim Square**, dominated by the terminus of an underground system that runs to the business districts such as 4 Levent. The tall building on the right is the five-star **Marmara Hotel**, which affords a superb view of the city from its rooftop bar. The modern building on the eastern side is the **Atatürk Cultural Centre** (box office tel: (0212) 2515600), where most of the city's opera performances and concerts take place.

Taksim Park stands across from the Etap Marmara. The statue in the square, **Taksim Anıtı**, commemorates the founding of the Turkish Republic, erected in 1928. Airline offices line **Cumhuriyet Caddesi** (Republic Avenue), the street that runs north of Taksim Park to the modern shopping neighbourhoods of **Nisantaşı**, **Osmanbey** and **Şişli**, as well as to **Conference Valley**. This houses the **Hilton Hotel**, the **Lütfi Kırdar Centre**, the **Açik Hava** (open air) **Theatre** and the **Military Museum** (tel: (0212) 2332720; open Wed–Sun 9am–5pm), in the grand military academy where Atatürk trained. A segment of the museum is devoted to the Turkish hero, and it has a fascinating range of exhibits from medieval Ottoman tents and armour onwards. Every afternoon, a mehter janissary band plays in the courtyard.

Return to Taksim Square and take the funicular down the hill. From the bottom, it's a few minutes' walk or one stop on the tram to **Dolmabahçe Palace** (Oct–Feb 9am–3pm, Mar–Sept 9am–4pm, closed Mon and Thur; guided tours only; entrance fee). The entrance is through a monumental gateway leading into a courtyard, and regular guided tours are available. The three-storey palace was built in 1854 by Nikogos Balyan, who collaborated with his father, Karabet. The sultans borrowed heavily from foreign banks and emptied the state coffers to build the lavish 600-metre (650-yd) residence, which was intended to surpass its European counterparts in magnificence and opulence. Dolmabahçe Palace served as the principal imperial residence until Abdül Hamit, sensing the end was nigh, moved to Yıldız Palace on the hill above Beşiktaş. In the last years of the empire, Dolmabahçe

Left: entertaining the tourists

was used solely for ceremonial purposes and state receptions, and the gardens have that function today. Kemal Atatürk used it as a presidential residence and died here, officially, on 10 November 1938.

Facing the sea, the palace has a central building flanked by two wings, housing the State Room and the royal household. It has more than 285 rooms, 43 large salons and six balconies, as well as the biggest crystal chandelier in the world, which hangs from the roof in the **State Room**. The centre-piece of the palace, however, is the ornate, curved staircase leading to the **Salon of the Ambassadors**, the imperial reception room, with its crystal and marble balusters. All clocks in the palace are set to the exact time that Atatürk died, and his deathbed is draped with a Turkish flag. Ask your guide to show you **Atatürk's Room** (in the former Harem).

The secretariat and the parliamentary assembly of the Black Sea Economic Cooperation (BSEC, an 11-nation trade pact formed in 1992 between Turkey, Albania, Bulgaria, Greece, Romania and six former Soviet republics) are located in the Harekât Kiosk, one of several ornate buildings in the palace grounds.

Right next door to the Dolmabahçe are the **Naval Museum** (*see page 46*) and the **Museum of Painting and Sculpture** (open Tue–Sat 10am–4.30pm), a rich collection of 19th- and 20th-century Turkish art.

Evening Entertainment

From Dolmabahçe Palace, you can take a taxi or *dolmuş* to **Taksim Square** for the evening. In Beyoğlu today, as in the Pera of the past, you are spoilt for choice, and can round off your day with a visit to the rooftop bars of any of the city's five-star hotels, one of the numerous pâtisseries which line Istiklâl, the techno club behind St Antoine's, or the 'approved' belly dancing spots, most of which are near the Hilton Hotel on Cumhuriyet Caddesi. Keep away from the seedy dives found down back alleys, and the touts that might try to lure you. Otherwise you run serious risk of losing your entire holiday budget to the whiskey dollies and their keepers inside, and even the police cannot help you. You have been warned.

Above: the view from the Galata Tower

5. AROUND THE COVERED BAZAAR *(see map, below)*

Begin at Çemberlitaş; see the Column of Constantine and the Köprülü Mehmet Paşa Complex; visit the Nuruosmaniye and Mahmut Paşa Mosques, explore the Vezir Hanı and the other silk road inns of Ottoman times, and shop till you drop in the Covered Bazaar.

Start your morning at **Çemberlitaş**, a noisy, crowded district on the tramline 600 metres/yds west of Sultanahmet Park. **Yeniçeriler Caddesi**, a continuation of Divanyolu, runs on an east-west axis from Sultanahmet. It means 'hooped column' in Turkish, a name derived from the blackened remains of the **Column of Constantine** which stands on the north side. Byzantine scribes suggest that it may have been pre-Christian in origin. The forum itself was surrounded by two-storey porticoes, which contained a senate building along with Christian and pagan statues.

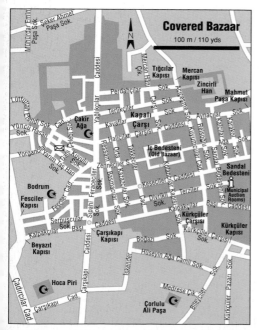

The building you see diagonally across the street is the 17th-century **Köprülü Mehmet Paşa Complex** with its mosque and *medrese* (theological school), established by a member of an illustrious dynasty of grand viziers who served in the 17th and 18th centuries. Köprülü Mehmet Paşa is buried in a cemetery in the courtyard, as is Fuat

Above: all that glisters in the Covered Bazaar

Köprülü (1890–1966), a recent family member and Ottoman historian who served as foreign minister in the 1950s.

Atik Ali Paşa Camii is one of the oldest mosques in the city, built in 1496 during the reign of Beyazıt II by his eunuch grand vizier. There is a tea garden on the premises specialising in 'mystic water pipe smoking' – the traditional Turkish *nargile*, which contains scented tobacco. Now turn left on Vezirhanı Caddesi. On your right is the **Çemberlitaş Hamamı**, (6am–midnight). Built in 1583 to a plan of Sinan, this bath is recommended.

About five minutes further down Vezirhanı, the **Nuruosmaniye** and **Mahmut Paşa Mosques** are both worth a look. The former was begun in 1748 and was the first to display the baroque features that were disapproved of by the clergy at the time. Note the unusual horseshoe-shaped courtyard, ornate exterior and curved sultan's ramp, and the *medrese*, now a students' dormitory. The latter was built in 1462 by Mahmut Paşa, a highly respected Byzantine aristocrat who converted to Islam and ultimately became grand vizier to Mehmet the Conqueror. He was executed in 1473, but fortunately his beautiful tomb had already been constructed, a striking but simple structure of turquoise, dark blue and green tiles from early Iznik kilns.

The Merchant Classes

The 17th-century **Vezir Hanı**, for which the street is named, is now severely dilapidated, but once served as lodging for visiting merchants, as did all the *hans* in this fascinating neighbourhood. **Valide Han** (Mon–Sat 9.30am–5pm) was built by Kösem Sultan in 1651 and was the centre of Persian trade in the city. By 1700 several thousand people, mostly from Azerbaijan, were living here, and this explains the Shi'ite mosque at the centre. Traditionally, animals and goods were stored at ground level and the itinerant merchants and craftsman stayed above. Today, most *hans* are nothing more than sweatshops, though it is still interesting to see them at work. Further down, the baroque **Büyük Yeni Han** has three levels of shops, joining many more *hans* and craftsmen's alleys which have been here for 500 years. **Süleyman Paşa Han** was the old slave market.

One of the main entrances to the **Covered Bazaar**, or **Kapalı Çarşı** (8.30am–7pm, closed Sun), the world's biggest emporium, is at the southwestern end of the Nuruosmaniye Mosque arcade. The oldest part, the fortress-like Iç Bedestan, is at the centre of an oriental labyrinth of passageways and corridors with 64 streets, 3,000 shops, 22 entrances, 25,000 employees, four fountains and two mosques, 17 inns and 10 wells. Here is where you'll find jewellery, carpets, antiques (real and repro), ceramics, leatherware, shoes, furniture, alabaster, copper and tin products, silk fabrics, curtains, and designer fakes. Rents have become steep and, sadly, the goods less exotic, relying on rapid turnover, but you can still find treasures if you take the time, and haggle expertly.

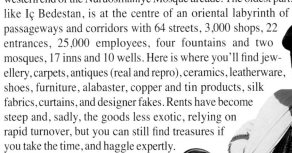

Between 250,000 and 400,000 people shop there every day, including locals, foreigners, and

Right: hawker on Beyazıt Square

'luggage' traders from former Soviet countries. To avoid getting lost in its maze-like streets, always return to its main vaulted street, **Kalpakçılar Başı Caddesi (Avenue of the Head Kalpak maker)** which runs through the Bazaar in an east-west direction and shimmers with gold earrings, bracelets, rings and chains. Most trades remain grouped together – as they were 530 years ago, and the centre of goldsmithing is the Cuhaza Han, which contains over 300 ateliers, as well as nine gold-smelting forges and scores of wholesale outlets.

As you walk in an east-west direction along Kalpakçılar Başı Caddesi, you will notice **Sandal Bedesteni**, an enclosed area which was added in the 16th century and which has been recently restored. Visit on Monday and Thursday at 1pm when hand-made carpets are auctioned.

Turn right and walk down the second street that intersects Kalpakçılar Başı Caddesi, **Kuyumcular Caddesi**. The curious two-storey structure in the middle of the street is a former one-cubicle mosque, now a jewellery shop. Return to the Covered Bazaar along Ağa Sokak and enter the **Old Bazaar**, **Eski Bedesteni**, one of the most dazzling sections of the emporium with its jewellers, antiques dealers and carpet sellers.

6. AROUND SARAY BURNU (see map, page 68)

Visit the Archaeology Museum, the Museum of the Ancient Orient and the Tiled Kiosk Museum; take a stroll through Gülhane Parkı; walk up the Golden Horn. Explore Yeni Camii mosque and the Spice Bazaar and have lunch at Pandeli's Restaurant.

Your morning begins at 9am with visits to the **Archaeology Museum**, the **Museum of the Ancient Orient**, and the **Tiled Kiosk Museum**, which contains collections of 16th-century ceramics (all open Tue–Sun 8.30am–5pm; single entrance fee). The three are situated together around a courtyard, between the First Court of Topkapı Palace and Gülhane Parkı.

The Archaeological Museum was founded in 1881 by Osman Hamdi Bey, the son of a grand vizier, one of Turkey's first archaeologists, and an activist in his efforts to stop the export of antiquities from the Empire. Two major finds necessitated the building of the current museum, which now houses one of the finest collections of classical and pre-classical artefacts found anywhere in the world. The centrepiece is the splendid **Alexander Sarcophagus**, found during excavations at the royal necropolis of Sidon in Lebanon. The sarcophagus did not belong to Alexander but to an admirer, possibly one of his generals, and gets its name from the friezes depicting the legendary leader fighting with the Greek army against the Persians. Nearby is the equally impressive **Sarcophagus of Mourners**, shaped like a Greek temple, with friezes of crying

Above: an Aladdin's Cave

women and Alexander depicted in a hunting scene. Inside the entrance you are greeted by the contorted face of the Egyptian god Bes, meant to scare away evil spirits. Exhibits include a mummified Egyptian king, a number of Roman statues, remnants of Byzantine Constantinople, such as a snake head from the Serpentine Column in the Hippodrome, lions from Bucoleon Palace, and a rare 7th-century mosaic that survived the iconoclastic era. One room is devoted to the mysterious Phrygians, and includes an 8th-century-BC tomb with its grave goods intact; items from excavations at Troy; a copy of the façade of the Temple of Athena at Assos and some 3rd century-BC figures of chubby boy temple prostitutes that were taken from a shrine of Aphrodite in Cyprus.

World's Oldest Peace Treaty

The Museum of the Ancient Orient, the first building in the courtyard, contains a unique collection of Babylonian, Sumerian, Hittite and Egyptian artefacts, including more than 70,000 Sumerian and Arcadian cuneiform tablets, of which the **Treaty of Kadesh** is the most famous. Signed in 1269BC between the Egyptian pharaoh and the Hittite King Hattusilis III, it is the earliest known peace treaty in the world. The collection of 13th-century BC sarcophagi with pharaohs' heads is equally impressive. One of these coffins holds the mummified bodies of Bak-N-Mutand and his sacred cat.

A pleasant outdoor coffee house, lined with Greek columns and sarcophagi and sycamore trees, stands between the Museum of Ancient Orient and the **Tiled Kiosk Museum** or **Çinili Köşk**, which houses ceramics and mosque lamps from the finest years of Iznik production. The Tiled Kiosk is one of the few buildings left from the time of Mehmet II, but it was never a residence – the sultan used this pavilion as a place to relax from administrative pressures, the tiled walls providing respite from the heat.

Above: the Alexander sarcophagus
Right: standing guard outside the Museum of Oriental Antiques

After a quick tour of the museums walk downhill to **Gülhane Parkı**, once a part of the gardens of Topkapı Palace, but today a rather downmarket funfair. Step out of the massive gates on your left briefly – the building you see across the street (**Alemdar Caddesi**) is the **State Security Court**, where political cases are tried. The building served until recently as the city morgue. The ornate gate you see to the right is the back entrance to the **Provincial Capitol**, formerly the Sublime Porte, which opened into the **Offices of the Grand Vizier** during Ottoman times.

Shooting Spy

Return to the park. The building on your left, on top of the palace wall overlooking the street below, is the **Alay Köşkü** or Parade Pavilion, from which the sultan could spy unseen on comings and goings at the Porte, as well as enjoy a ringside seat for official and military processions. Alemdar means 'standard bearer', and one 17th-century scribe noted the colourful Parade of the Guilds, with each section dressed in the costumes of their trade along with mime actors and other circus acts. During his rule in the early 17th century, Ibrahim the Mad used the kiosk as a vantage point from which to shoot pedestrians entering the Sublime Porte with his crossbow.

As you walk through Gülhane Parkı you will see Istanbul's only zoo on your left, although it is unlikely to impress. To your right, near the entrance to the park, are the busts of some of the former mayors of Istanbul. The tiny **Tanzimat Museum** (9.30am–4.30pm), which is further on to your right, displays the **Noble Rescript of the Rose Chamber**, the most important document of 19th-century Tanzimat reforms. The decree, as proclaimed by the sultan in 1839 at this very spot, was a Bill of Rights granting all Ottoman citizens security of life, honour, property rights and equality of all religions in the application of Ottoman laws.

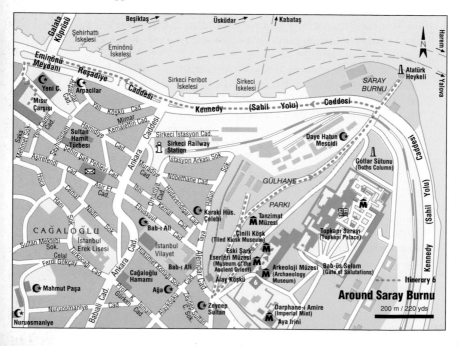

The building that towers over the inner wall of Topkapı Palace to your right is part of the Harem, the Kiosk of Osman III, sultan 1754–57. Near the end of the park, a trail leads to the **Goths Column**, built sometime between AD268 and 270 to celebrate Claudius II Gothicus's victory over the Goths. When you reach the end of the park, cross the railway and Kennedy Caddesi, named after John F Kennedy. You have now reached **Saray Burnu**, or **Palace Point**, at the confluence of the Golden Horn, the Bosphorus and the Sea of Marmara. A statue of Atatürk (1881–1938), founder and first president of the Turkish Republic, stands in the park, completed in 1926 by Austrian sculptor Heinrich Krippel.

Around the Golden Horn

From Saray Burnu, turn left, keep to the pavement, and follow the Golden Horn, or Haliç, an inlet of the Bosphorus, 8km long and 400 metres wide (5 miles by 400yds), where the city's harbour is located.

Once lined with palace gardens, public parks, churches and mosques, and described by poets as **Sadabad**, or place of bliss, the Golden Horn had in more recent years deteriorated into an open cesspool which smelled gaspingly dreadful, even from miles away. Efforts at cleaning and dredging the Horn, however, have met with some success. The municipality has demolished 1,200 buildings, including 400 polluting factories, and built new parks and playgrounds along its shores.

The first building you come to on your right is **Sepetçiler Kasrı**, or **Palace of the Basket Weavers**, a 17th-century building originally part of Topkapı Palace grounds. It is now the International Press Centre. The building takes its original name from the fact that the mad Sultan, Deli Ibrahim, spent long days sitting here weaving baskets – his favourite hobby. Across the street is the **Sirkeci Railway Station**, the terminus of the Orient Express train service, which once had horse-drawn carriages waiting outside to take new arrivals across the Horn to the Pera Palace. The famous service is the star of the recently opened **Railway Museum** (open Tue–Sat 9am–5pm), part of the restored station that now also offers both travellers and trainspotters an excellent restaurant and a healthy dose of nostalgia.

The old Galata Bridge, a pontoon crossing constructed in 1972, was dismantled and rebuilt further up the Golden Horn after suffering damage in a fire. The main ferry landings are to your right, and you soon come to the new bridge, not a patch on its predecessor, although it has helped to ease Istanbul's traffic.

Above: a carpet seller in Behramkale

city itineraries

Take the underpass and cross the street to **Yeni Camii**, or the **New Mosque**, a 17th-century shrine whose grey hulk squats over the bustling commercial district of Eminönü. Its courtyard is always host to an army of pigeons, fed by generous visitors, earning it the sobriquet, 'Pigeon Mosque'. A square room, canopied by a central dome and four semi-domes, has pretty blue-and-white tiles on its interior walls. Next to it is the famous **Mısır Çarşışı**, or **Egyptian Bazaar** (8am–7pm, closed Sun), built in 1660 (and restored in 1940) to pay for the mosque and once one of the biggest spice markets in the world.

Spice Bazaar

Mısır, in Turkish, means both corn and Egypt, as it was from Egypt that spices, grains, pulses, coffee, incense and henna came in great abundance, arriving annually in a convoy of galleons to great fanfare, and accompanied by warships to protect them from pirates. Get to the bazaar early, if you can, around 9am, to avoid the touts and tourist hordes. A handful of traditional spice sellers remain (such as **Ücuzcular** at No 51), and their array of goods is astonishing, with more than 3,000 spices, hundreds of flower essences and specially-made cosmetic creams.

For lunch, the hot and foot-weary may choose the famous and reasonably-priced **Pandeli's Restaurant**, upstairs from the main entrance of the bazaar. It has fairly uninspired international cuisine but it is very convenient and has a wonderfully cool interior, resulting from the historic floor-to-ceiling

turquoise tiles. If the tourist hassle gets too much, simply follow the streets – and your nose – around Hasırcılar and Tahtakale Caddesi where many of the less well-known spice sellers, *kahvecis* (coffee grinders) and makers of *pastırma* (dried, spiced beef) have moved. Further out towards Uzunçarşı you will find a warren of old craftsmen's workshops – coppersmiths, wood-workers and many more.

The farmer's market at Tahmis Caddesi is one of the best in town, and if you walk along the front of Kalçın Sokak, where the shops face the sea (and a bus station) you come to **Hamdi's**. This is one of Istanbul's best kept secrets as it is one of the city's nicest and cheapest restaurants, serving authentic eastern Turkish cuisine.

Above : in the Spice Bazaar
Left: outside the New Mosque

7. STUDENT DAYS *(see map, page 72)*

Begin at Sahaflar Çarşışı, the old booksellers' market off the Covered Bazaar; pass through Beyazıt Camii and Beyazıt Square; stroll through the campus of Istanbul University and then make your way into the magnificent Süleymaniye Mosque complex.

Start at the **Old Book Bazaar** or **Sahaflar Çarşışı**, a booksellers' market since the 18th century, just off the western exit of the Covered Bazaar. There are some notable antiquarian bookshops here, but most simply deal in textbooks and secondhand paperbacks.

The back of the courtyard leads to a flea market, best at weekends when there's a good combination of junk and Central Asian embroideries, and on to **Beyazıt Square**, once the Byzantine Forum of Theodosius. Ahead of you are the imposing gates of **Istanbul University**.

Beyazıt Camii is on your left, the oldest surviving imperial mosque in Istanbul, completed in 1506 as part of the old palace complex. It is thought to reflect the austere and pious nature of the Conqueror's son, and also to mark the beginning of a distinctive Ottoman architectural style – both subtle and symmetrical. Note the 20 verd antique, red granite and porphyry columns, and the *türbes* (tombs) of Sultan Beyazıt II (sultan 1481–1512), his daughter Selçuk Sultan, and Grand Vizier Koca Resit Paşa, the leader of the Tanzimat reform movement, who died in 1857. The mosque's *medrese* is now the

Museum of Calligraphy (Türk Vakıf Hat Sanatları Müzesi; 9am–4pm, closed Sun and Mon), which has an excellent exhibition from the archives of the Turkish Calligraphy Foundation.

Beyazıt Square is in front of the main campus of Istanbul University, one of the country's great institutions of learning, and the site of many student demonstrations over the years. In the early part of the last century women protested here against having to wear headscarves, and some, today, are protesting to put them back on again. The campus is on the grounds of Mehmet II's first palace, later the Ministry of War, and **Beyazıt Tower**, a fire watchtower and meteorology station, is by the main building.

Walk along the outer western walls of the university to the **Süleymaniye Mosque Complex** of Süleyman the Magnificent (sultan 1520–66), a testimony to the most revered and cultured ruler of the Ottoman Empire. It was completed in 1557, after only seven years, by the great Ottoman architect Mimar Sinan, and is considered his masterpiece.

Süleyman and his beloved wife Roxelana had moved to Topkapı Palace, so half the imperial gardens of the old palace on the Third Hill were requisitioned. Roxelana, 'the Russian' had such a hold over the sultan that she eventually persuaded him to kill his son, Mustafa, on the pretext that he was planning to usurp the throne, thus enabling her own son, Selim the Sot, to succeed. Many historians date the decline of the grand Ottoman Empire back to Selim's weak and alcoholic rule.

Right: selling old titles at the Old Book Bazaar

The mosque's dome stands 47 metres (156ft) above the ground, and the tile work and stained glass are exquisite. The calligraphy in the domes and pendatives was carried out by one of the finest artists of the period, and the four minarets are traditionally said to represent Süleyman's status as fourth sultan. The mosque is surrounded by a vast outer courtyard flanked on three sides by a wall with grilled windows, and preceded by a porticoed *avlu* (court-yard). Its 24 columns are thought to have been salvaged from the Byzantine royal box at the hippodrome.

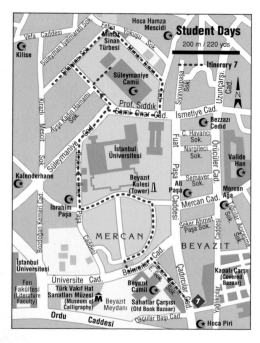

In the cemetery are the **tombs of Süleyman and Roxelana** and further along lies the tomb of the architect himself. If you are looking for a break after a day's walk, take note of the **Darüzziyafe** Ottoman restaurant (Şifahane Caddesi 6, no alcohol) previously a soup kitchen and banqueting hall part of the original complex, along with the **Ikram** teahouse in a sunken garden on the left.

The area surrounding the complex is a dense warren of crumbling wooden houses, student teahouses and decaying Ottoman fountains.

Above: the interior of the Süleymaniye Mosque

8. A RELIGIOUS WALKWAY *(see map, page 74)*

Tour the upper reaches of the Golden Horn, starting from Rüstem Paşa Camii. Visit the Orthodox Church Patriarchate, the old Greek neighbourhood of Fener and the old Jewish neighbourhood of Balat. Then take a taxi to Kariye Camii; walk the Byzantine Land Walls to Tekfur Sarayı, the Palace of Blachernae, the Walls of Leo and Heraclius and finally the Holy Ayazma.

Begin at Hasırcılar Caddesi, 100 metres (110yds) from the Spice Market to visit the **mosque of Rüstem Paşa**, considered by many to be the loveliest in all Istanbul. It was built by Mimar Sinan in 1561 in memory of Rüstem Paşa, twice grand vizier under Süleyman the Magnificent and husband of the sultan's favourite daughter, Mihrimah Sultan.

An expert at filling imperial coffers, Rüstem Paşa died in office of natural causes – quite unusual for grand viziers. But he is also remembered for having conspired with Mihrimah and Roxclana (Hürrem Sultan, Mihrimah's mother) to get the previous grand vizier, Ibrahim Paşa, strangled. The mosque, built on a high terrace over a complex of shops, is lavishly decorated with the finest Iznik tiles. These are worth studying: some colours were never again reproduced in Iznik kilns and many of the best are in the galleries.

Now head for Ragıp Gümüşpala Caddesi, the highway that runs along the Golden Horn. You will see two old commercial buildings or *hans*, the bigger of which is **Zindan Han**, or Prison Han, once a women's prison but now a tourist shopping centre with a top-floor restaurant that has a fine panoramic view of Istanbul harbour.

Byzantine-built Aqueduct

On the sea side is the **Ahi Çelebi Mosque**, built in the 15th century. You soon come to the **Atatürk Bridge**, spanning the Golden Horn, and on the hill to your left is the 4th-century **Aqueduct of Valens**, a superb feat of Byzantine engineering built in AD375 and still functioning at the end of the

19th century. Originally 1km (over half a mile) long, it brought water from mountains up to 200km (124 miles) away and flowed into a nymphaeum at the Forum Tauri (now Beyazıt Square). Today about half of it remains, towering over the traffic on Atatürk Boulevard. In the square beside it stands the **Fatih Memorial**, a modern equestrian statue of Mehmet the Conqueror and his companions.

Past the bridge, parts of the Byzantine sea walls remain intact. In the water, a huge fountain gushes on what was once the playground of the Ottoman aristocracy. It has a more useful purpose, however. For years, the Golden Horn was little more than a stinking cesspit and it took a multi-million dollar cleanup to bring it back to life. The fountain now helps oxygenate the water – like a giant

Above: Valens Aqueduct

fish tank. If you look across the Golden Horn, you can see the **Camialtı and Taskızak Shipyards**, which have been here for more than 500 years.

The palatial white building near the shore was the Ministry of War, later the Regional Navy Command, and the building on the hill the Naval Hospital. The navy moved out in 2007, and the future of the whole complex will almost certainly involve at least one five-star hotel.

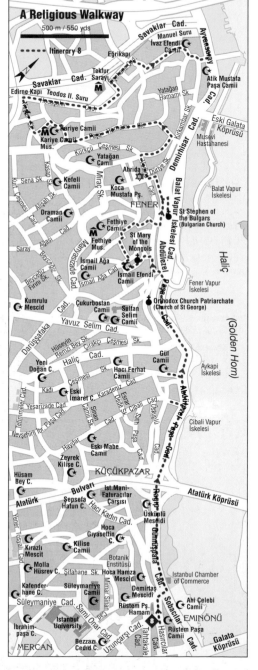

You soon come to **Çibali Kapısı**, one of the principal sea gates of the Byzantine walls. It gets its name from Çebe Ali Bey, one of Mehmet II's officers, whose troops breached the wall here during the Ottoman conquest in 1453. Roughly 270 metres (300yds) on is **Aya Nikola**, the 18th-century church of St Nicholas. It was originally the *metochion*, or private property, of the Vatopedi Monastery on Mount Athos in northeastern Greece.

Beyond Aya Nikola is the Aya Kapısı, the **Holy Gate**. Enter the gate and the second street on the left takes you to the imposing **Gül Camii**, or Mosque of Roses, formerly the Orthodox **Church of St Theodosia** at Mektep Sok. The church was built in the 9th century by Basil I, but the original dedication to St Euphemia was quickly overshadowed by the popularity of the martyred St Theodosia who had led the mostly female riot against iconoclast Leo III, when he smashed the icon of Christ above the gate to the Great Palace.

The last Byzantine Emperor, Constantine XI Dragases, said his final prayers here the night before the conqueror broke through the walls. The Ottomans used it as

Top Right: a quiet street in Fener
Right: enjoying a waterpipe

a naval storage depot until the 17th century, when it became a mosque.

Back along the waterfront, continuing up the Golden Horn, you reach the district of **Fener** (Phanar) and the **Orthodox Church Patriarchate**, which has been on this site since 1601. Considering that it is the symbolic spiritual centre of the world's 200 million Orthodox Christians the Patriarchate is a modest establishment, fearing to attract controversy, and with good reason. From Fener, the Patriarch wields influence over Orthodox churches in Crete, the Dodecanese Islands, the monastic community of Mount Athos in Greece, the US, Canada, Australia, New Zealand, South America and Western Europe.

Entrance to the Patriarchate is by **Sadrazam Ali Paşa Caddesi** just off Abdülezel Paşa Caddesi, the street that runs along the Golden Horn. The main gate **Orta Kapı**, or Central Door, is welded shut and painted black, as this was the spot where Patriarch Gregory V was hanged for treason on Easter Sunday, 1821, at the start of the Greek War of Independence from the Ottoman Empire. His body was left hanging for three days as warning to Greek nationalist factions among the parishioners, before being thrown into the sea.

A Corner of Greece

The **Church of St George** dates from 1720. Above its main entrance is a two-headed eagle with its wings spread, one holding the cross and the other holding a crown, representing the spiritual and temporal powers of the Patriarch and the Byzantine emperors. Icons inside the cavern-like church are darkened from the soot of candles. The most impressive item is a gold mosaic of the Virgin Mary and Christ. The sarcophagi of several early saints are along the southern wall.

Once a flourishing Greek neighbour-hood, Fener has decayed, but still contains many Greek churches and buildings of interest. Greek families resident here since the 16th century, known as the Phenariots, amassed huge fortunes from trade and commerce and wielded considerable influence on the Ottoman Empire's foreign affairs. They acquired high positions, becoming *de facto* governors of the Aegean Islands,which provided crews for the Ottoman navy. The most influential position, however, was that of *hospodar*, or lord, of the Danubian principalities of Moldavia and Walachia, and the wealth acquired from these territories was channelled back to Fener, financing palaces and luxurious homes, traces of which can still be seen.

On the same street as the Patriarchate, 45 metres (50yds) to the northeast, is the palatial özel Maraşlı Rum Ilkokulu, a Greek primary school. If you walk uphill along the narrow, cobbled streets, you'll reach the **Greek High School of Fener**, a red-brick, castle-like building towering over the neighbourhood. Known as the **Megali Scolio**, or Grand School, it was one of the great Greek secular schools of learning in the Ottoman Empire. Today, only a handful of students remain. A bust of Kemal Atatürk, who vanquished the invading Greek army during the Turkish War of Independence (1919–22), stands in the courtyard of the school, now under the authority of the Turkish Ministry of Education.

St Mary of the Mongols

Of the existing Greek churches in Fener **St Mary of the Mongols** (Sun only) or the Mouchliotissa, west of the Greek National School, is most impressive. Established in 1282 by Princess Maria Peleogina, an illegitimate daughter of Byzantine Emperor Michael Palaeologus (1261–82), the church is noted for its unique high drum, pink-coloured exterior and darkened icons.

Maria first marriage to Holagu, a Khan of the Mongols, was arranged by the sovereign to remove the Mongol threat. She became known as Despoina (mistress) of the Mongols, when, on her way to meet her husband in Caesarea (modern-day Kayseri, in central Anatolia), word came that the Khan was dead, and she continued to the Mongolian court and married Holagu's son and successor, Abaga. When he was murdered 16 years later, Maria returned to Constantinople and was again married to a Mongol prince, Charbanda, to ensure his support in thwarting the Ottoman menace facing the Byzantine state. St Mary of the Mongols, is the oldest surviving Byzantine church still under the control of the Patriarchate.

Above: reading the Torah, Balat Synagogue

A 10-minute walk back to the Golden Horn brings you to one of the most unusual buildings in Istanbul: **St Stephen of the Bulgars**, made completely from cast iron. It was cast in Vienna in 1871 and shipped down the Danube in sections. Though currrently closed for restoration, it still serves Istanbul's tiny Bulgarian community. The church is in the middle of the park between two avenues. From her to Eyüp, most of this bank of the Golden Horn is lined by parkway popular with joggers, dog walkers and children.

About 250 metres (274yds) past the Bulgarian Church is the **Metochion of Mount Sinai**, a semi-autonomous church under the control of the Patriarchate of Egypt, also responsible for St Catherine's Monastery on Mount Sinai. The Archimandrite, or leader, was expelled from Turkey and the building confiscated by the government in retaliation to Nasser's nationalisation of Turkish properties in Egypt in the 1950s.

Jewish District

The next neighbourhood along the upper reaches of the Golden Horn is **Balat**, one of the principal districts settled by the Jewish community, which has been here since the time of Alexander the Great, swelling at the end of the 15th century with the expulsion of Jews from Spain. Welcomed by the sultan, they quickly became influential diplomats and merchants. Though numbers have dwindled, many still live in Balat, which has several synagogues.

Ahrida is the oldest, in the centre of Balat, just off the main Golden Horn road. The synagogue was built before the Turkish conquest, and has an unusual altar shaped like an ark. Nearby is the Armenian **Church of Surp** (Saint) **Hiresdagbetermeni**, constructed in 1835, and **Feruh Kuthuda Camii**, a 16th-century mosque built by Sinan.

Balat is a Turkish corruption of the word *palation*, meaning palace, and is derived from Blachernae Palace, the last residence of the Byzantine emperors, traces of which can be seen along the Byzantine land walls. You will walk along these walls later.

Hail a taxi to your next destination, **Kariye Camii**, the Church of St Saviour in Chora (9am–5pm, closed Wed), near **Edirne Kapı**, one of the main gates along the Byzantine land walls. After Aya Sophia, Kariye Camii is the most fascinating church in Istanbul because of its brilliant mosaics and frescoes portraying the lives of Christ and the Virgin Mary. These are some the finest examples of Christian art in the world.

The church's Greek name, *Chora*, means 'in the country', as it was outside the first city walls built by Constantine the Great. The present church, built by the mother-in-law of the Byzantine Emperor Alexius I Comnenus, dates from the late 11th century, and the frescoes and paintings from the early 14th century by Grand Logethete Theodore Metochites, whose mosaic stands in the mural above the door to the nave. It shows him offering the church to the enthroned Christ.

Above: Chora mosaic

In the early 16th century, the Turks converted the church into a mosque, covering the paintings and mosaics with plaster. But the artwork has been restored and now Kariye Camii is a museum. Its surroundings have also been spruced up by the Automobile and Touring Association, who built the pleasant **Kariye Hotel** and the Kariye Café, which includes the authentic, old Turkish Muhallebici Salonu or **Pudding Shop**. You may wish to book a table at the atmospheric **Asithane Restaurant**, which specialises in Ottoman cuisine, for tonight's dinner.

There are more than 100 mosaics and frescoes in Kariye Camii. The mosaics are arranged in the following six groups and, in order to get the most from your visit, should be viewed in the right order:

• the six large dedicatory or devotional panels in the outer narthex and inner narthex, which include the **Portraits of SS Paul and Peter** (to the left and right of the nave) and the **Deesis** of Christ and the Virgin Mary;

• the genealogy of Christ in the northern and southern domes of the inner narthex, including a medallion of **Christ Pantocrator and His Ancestors**;

• the cycle of the Blessed Virgin in the first three bays of the inner narthex;

• the cycle of the infancy of Christ, which includes the stunning **Three Wise Men**. Each of the 13 mosaics occupies a mural in the outer narthex;

• the cycle of Christ's ministry occupying the domed vaults of all seven bays of the outer narthex as well as parts of the south bay of the inner narthex;

• the panels in the Nave, which include the **Dormition of the Virgin**, portraying the Virgin Mary aparently dead. Christ stands behind holding her soul, represented as a babe in swaddling clothes. Apostles, evangelists and early bishops of the church surround them. Hovering over the scene are six angels.

The frescoes are in the **Parecclesion**, a kind of enclosed aisle to the right of the church. These show:

• scenes from the resurrection, including the **Anastasis** (the Harrowing

Above: Christ with Adam and Eve, fresco at St Saviour in Chora

of Hell) one of the greatest paintings in the world. This shows Christ breaking the gates of Hell, which lie beneath his feet, while Satan lies bound before him. With his right hand he pulls Adam from his tomb. Behind Adam stand St John the Baptist, David, Solomon and other biblical kings. With his left he pulls Eve out of her tomb, in which stands Abel;

• The Last Judgment with scenes from heaven and hell;
• 27 saints and the martyrs.

A number of tombs exist in the walls of the Pareeclesion, including that of Theodore Metochites, traces of which can still be seen.

Byzantine City Walls

Leave the church and walk up to the Byzantine city walls, and follow them down the hill towards the Golden Horn. You will see a small section of the land walls, which are 19km (11 miles) long, extending from the Sea of Marmara to the Golden Horn. Most are now in ruins, although three gates and some stretches have been restored, but for more than 1,000 years they kept out invaders, until breached by the crusaders in 1204 and by the Ottoman Turks 250 years later. The land walls were 5 metres (16ft) thick and towered 12 metres (40ft) above the city, guarded by 96 towers. The Byzantines built magnificent houses and palaces along the walls, sadly all but disappeared.

As you walk down the hill, the first sight is the **Tekfur Sarayı**, or **Palace of the Sovereign**, possibly an appendage to Blachernae Palace. Only the façade of the building, erected between the late 13th and early 14th centuries, remains. After the Turkish conquest it became a zoo where the sultans kept the exotic animals given as gifts, hence the name of the neighbourhood, 'Ayvansaray', or animal castle. Now a shady, traditional neighbourhood of cobbled gardens and old wooden houses, it is one of the most pleasant strolls Istanbul can offer, although it is rarely visited by tourists.

Eğrikapı, or **Crooked Gate**, is one of many gates along the walls, and this one takes its name from the narrow lane which enters the city and must skirt around a mausoleum in front of the gate. Another 200 metres (220yds) downhill is the late 16th-century **Ivaz Efendi Camii**, the site on which the Byzantine **Palace of Blachernae** once stood, but only traces of the palace remain. If the mosque is open, have a look – though tiny, it purports to be a work of Sinan and does contain lovely Iznik tiles.

The tower behind the mosque has a bloody history, as it was where deposed emperors were imprisoned and tortured, often with their eyes put out. You may have to ask a caretaker to gain access to the far end of the mosque court by the tower, where a dangerous, crumbling stairway drops nearly

Right: parts of the city's Byzantine walls remain intact

100 metres/yds. The terrace teahouse to the right of the mosque gives a spectacular view of the end of the Byzantine walls and the upper reaches of the Golden Horn, and is a great place to pause for a rest.

If you continue your walk down the hill, following the land walls, you will soon arrive at the impressive red-brick **Walls of Leo and Heraclius** identifiable by their massive towers. Between the walls is a citadel, in which you can see a small Muslim graveyard.

9. THE HOLY DISTRICT OF EYÜP *(see map, page 18–19)*

Begin at the Eyüp Mosque; visit mausoleums and the complexes of Mihrişah Sultan and Zal Mahmut; head up to Pierre Loti's Coffeehouse for afternoon tea; walk down through the Eyüp cemetery.

Eyüp was a town created outside of Constantinople by the Conqueror, who encouraged settlers from Anatolia and Bursa attracted by proximity to the holy mausoleum of **Eyüp Al-Ansari**, a standard bearer of the Prophet Muhammed killed during the first Arab siege of Constantinople in AD688.

His burial place was discovered some eight centuries later, after being miraculously revealed in a dream to Mehmet II's Şeyh ül-Islam, or religious judge.

After Mecca, Medina and Jerusalem, **Eyüp Mosque** vies with Damascus and Kerbala as the fourth most important place of pilgrimage in the Islamic world, and the neighbourhood is solemn and devout as a result. Avoid visiting on a Friday, the principal day of worship, dress appropriately and do not take photos of women wearing full black çarşaf (veils).

Mehmet II ordered the construction of the first mosque complex, which includes the mausoleum, mosque, *medrese*, *han*, *hamam*, *imaret* and market, in 1458. By the 18th century, however, the complex was in ruins and Sultan Selim III had a new building erected in 1798.

Family Outings

The current **Eyüp Camii** (Cami-i Kebir Sokak) is baroque, and the shrine of Eyüp himself is lit up in green lights, the holy colour of the Prophet. It is here that Istanbul families bring their young boys, decked in spangled capes and caps, before ritual circumcision, and on weekends it is fun to watch newlyweds attend the mosque after their secular weddings, to be blessed by the imam. Religious brides negotiate the fashions of East and West by wearing the classic white gown, but with a matching headscarf.

In the hills overlooking Eyüp are sprawling shanty towns and the large **Eyüp Cemetery**, filled with old Ottoman tombs. It is still considered a privilege to be buried here. Behind Eyüp Mosque, facing the Golden Horn, is the **Complex of Mihrişah Valide Sultan**, a gigantic *külliye* built in 1794 and which includes the mausoleum of the founder, a *mektep* (primary school),

Above: young candidates for ritual circumcision
Top Right: inside the Pierre Loti coffeehouse. **Right:** in Eyüp Cemetery

an *imaret* (public kitchen), and splendid water fountains. Nearby is a series of *türbes*, including the **Mausoleum of Mehmet V Reşat**, sultan 1909–18. The tombs of several Ottoman Grand Viziers are located nearby, including the **Mausoleum of Sokollu Mehmet Paşa**. The son of a Bosnian priest, Mehmet Paşa was trained at the palace school and married Esmahan Sultan, daughter of Selim the Sot. An able statesman, he held many high positions, including that of grand vizier in the final years of Süleyman's reign. He was one of the main characters portrayed in Nobel Prize winner Ivo Andric's novel *The Bridge Over the Drina*.

From here walk to the **Mosque Complex of Zal Mahmut**, approximately 400 metres (437yds) to the northeast. Zal was an executioner, and one of those involved in the conspiracy led by Roxelana to have Prince Mustafa, son of Süleyman the Magnificent, put to death on trumped-up charges of treason. He later became a prominent official of substantial wealth and married the Princess Şah Sultan, another daughter of Selim the Sot, as a reward for his services. The mosque and courtyard are built on split levels, the lower holding the Türbes of Zal Mahmut and Princess Şah Sultan and a *medrese* (theological seminary). The mosque, together with another *medrese,* is on the upper levels.

Take a taxi to **Pierre Lotl's Coffeehouse** (8am–midnight) on the hill above Eyüp for afternoon tea. Loti (1850–1923), was a French naval officer and romantic writer who lived in Eyüp for several years and whose works lament the growing Europeanisation of Istanbul. Watch the sun set over the Golden Horn, then walk down the hill through the cemetery to view the unusual headstones with their turban-shaped tops.

Leisure Activities

SHOPPING

The best of Turkey's hand-woven wool and silk Anatolian carpets, leatherware, ceramics, gold and silver jewellery, modern miniatures, alabaster figurines, meerschaum pipes and antiques can be found in the Covered Bazaar, the biggest emporium in the world. As the market has become more touristy, prices have risen but are in line with other areas of the city. Bargaining is the norm.

A good rule of thumb is to start at about half the asking price. It also pays to shop around, as there's plenty of competition.

Leatherwear is everywhere in Aksaray and there are excellent factory outlets in Zeytınburnu between the old city and the airport. The area around the Spice Bazaar is overflowing with items, from modern kitchenware to hand-turned wooden bowls and copper pans. In the Asmalımesıct area, which begins at the *pasaj* opposite Tünel tram stop, are small art galleries and old bookshops. Galipdede Sok, leading from Tünel to Galata Tower, has musical instrument and CD shops, and the famous Librairie de Pera bookshop.

Istiklâl Caddesi in Beyoğlu is eclectic. Vakko is the most expensive and fashionable department store, and glassware, some handblown, at Paşabahçe's retail outlet is superb. This 3-km (2-mile) pedestrianised street teems with stores selling books in English old and new. Search back alleys and indoor passages for crafts, cut-rate designer fakes, jewellery, antiques and quirky CD shops.

The Çukurcuma area, near the Galatasaray Hamamı off Istiklâl, is full of antique and junk shops, and there are flea markets in Ortakoy and Kadiköy on Sundays. The underground walkway in Karaköy and backstreets of Eminönü offer cut-price electrical goods (prices are lower than elsewhere in Europe), and the designer boutiques are in the fashionable neighbourhoods of Teşvikye and Nişantaşı In Moda, Bağdat Caddesi is the Asian equivalent of Istiklâl, with high octane shops, restaurants and entertainment. Otherwise, the main shopping centres include the modern Galleria mall in Ataköy, near Atatürk International Airport, and the huge Kanyon Mall in Levent.

Even on Sundays and holidays when conventional shops are closed, the streets are crammed with people selling toys, cheap clothes, alarm clocks, pornography, popcorn and the very occasional precious antiques. Doing a deal has been the life and soul of Istanbul since the time of Constantine, and mercifully nothing has yet been done to 'regulate' it. All the same, be suspicious of anything sounding too cheap: rolls of film may have only three frames inside, most 'antiques' are reproductions and 'designer' bags are almost certain to have been made locally.

Carpets

Bazaar 54
54 Nuruosmaniye Cad.
Cağaloğlu
Tel: (0212) 5116500
One of the largest selections of silk and wool carpets in the world, as well as Turkey's biggest jewellery centre and extensive collections of souvenirs. Silk carpets are very expensive but a good investment (prices tend to be higher if you shop in a group).

Left: inside the covered bazaar
Right: carpets can be irresistible

Sengör Halıları
Takkeciler 65-75-83, Kapalıçarşı
Tel: (0212) 5272192/5224115
One of the oldest carpet sellers in the city.

Jewellery

The Brothers
Kapalıçarsı, Içbedesten
Şerifağa Sok. 30–31
Tel: (0212) 5284775
Hand-made Anatolian silver and gold jewellery. Prices are moderate.

Sema Paksoy
Atiye Sok. 9, Teşvikiye
Tel: (0212) 2193941
Gorgeous designs, combining old ethnic jewellery and dramatic chunks of stone with elegantly simple gold and silver settings.

Urart Sanat Galerisi
Abdi Ipekci Cad. 18/1 Nişantaşı
Tel: (0212) 2467194
Silver and gold jewellery as well as paintings and sculptures.

Department Stores

Vakko
Istiklâl Cad. 123–125, Beyoğlu
Tel: (0212) 2514092
The Harrods of Istanbul. Expensive, but worth a look. The gift-wrapping is exquisite.

Clothing

Beymen
Ak Merkez, Etiler
Tel: (0212) 2820380
Expensive top-quality clothing. There are other shops in the chain, including one at *Halâskargazi Cad No 230, Osmanbey.*

Souvenirs

Ali Muhiddin Hacı Bekir
Istiklal Cad. 129, Beyoğlu
Tel: (0212) 2442804
Hamidiye Cad. 83, Sirkeci
Tel: (0212) 5220666
King of Turkish Delight and other luscious edibles. In business since 1777.

Dösem
Off Bab-ı Hümayün Cad., Sultanahmet
Tel: (0212) 5133134
Sited opposite the entrance to the Topkapı Palace, this is the official Ministry of Culture shop, with high-quality products including historical replicas, wood, jewellery, silver and textiles at reasonable fixed prices.

Istanbul Handicrafts Centre
Kabasakal Cad. 7, Sultanahmet
Tel: (0212) 5176782
Once the *medrese* (religious school) of the Blue Mosque, this is now a market and workshop area, selling traditional crafts.

Kalmaz Baharat
Mısır Çarşısı 41/1, Eminönü
Tel: (0212) 5226604
Enticing stores in the Egyptian Market, specialising in spices, medicinal herbs and teas.

Les Arts Turcs
Incili Çavus Sok. 37, Kat. 3 Alemdar Mah.
Tel: (0212) 5207743
www.lesartsturcs.com
Wonderful gallery of Turkish arts and crafts behind the Yerebatan Sarayı entrance. Also design and create belly-dancing costumes.

Seyitağaoğulları Carpet Kilim Hand Crafts
Avrupa Pasajı 15, Meşrutiyet Cad. 16,
Galatasaray, Beyoğlu
Tel: (0212) 2492903
Arasta Çarşısı, Sultanahmet
Tel: (0212) 5169351
Items from bags to boots made from *kilim*.

Leatherware

Derimod
Akmerkez Mall, Nisbetiye Cad., Etiler
Tel: (0212) 2820668
Stylish leather jackets. Moderate prices.

Desa
Istiklal Caddesi, 140 Beyoğlu
Tel: (0212) 2433786
Wide range of products, from suitcases to belts, wallets and handbags. There are numerous branches of Desa across the city, plus an outlet branch (open 9am–7.30pm daily) at *Halkalı Caddesi, 208, Sefuköy, tel: (0212) 6989800.*

Ertuşrul
Valikonağı Caddesi, 101/A, Nişantaşı
Tel: (212) 2403052
Classic, durable ladies' shoes

Antiques, Art and Curios

Antik Palas
Spor Cad. Talimyeri Sok, Maçka
Tel: (0212) 2362460
Fourth-largest auction house in Europe. Specialises in Ottoman and European antiques.

Artrium I
Tünel Pasajı 5 &7
Tel: (0212) 2514302

Artrium II
Sofyalı Sok. 9, Tünel
Tel: (0212) 2514302, fax: (0212) 2498983
Ceramics, miniatures, calligraphy, prints and maps, paintings, textiles and jewellery.

Atlas Pasajı
Istiklâl Cad. 209, Beyoğlu
Entered through a historic cinema complex; this arcade is filled with everything from antiques to costumes and Central Asian jewellery; also alternative music stores.

Horhor Bit Pazarı (flea market)
Kırık Tulumba Sok, 13/22, Aksaray
A five-storey, upscale antiques market.

Izzet and Ipek Günay
Abide-i Hürriyet Cad., Tayyareci M. Ali Bey Sok. 12, Şişli, Tel: (0212) 2330717
Specialises in Ottoman antiques.

Ottomania
Sofyalı Sok. 30/32, Tünel
Tel: (0212) 2432157
Old engravings, calligraphy and maps.

Sofa
Nuruosmaniye Cad. 85
Tel: (0212) 5202850
Maps, miniatures, calligraphy and textiles.

Left: brassware in the Grand Bazaar
Above: ethnic hats of many colours

EATING OUT

Turkish food reflects the tastes of the Ottoman Empire, which stretched from Vienna to the deserts of Arabia. The Turkish palate favours the spicy kebabs of southern Anatolia, the tender lamb dishes of Central Asia, the steaks (*biftek* and *bonfile*) of Western Europe, and the *meze* (appetisers) of the Aegean and Mediterranean coasts.

Residents of Istanbul delight in the fish and seafood caught all along the Bosphorus and Marmara and Black seas. Some of the best catches in the area include *kalkan* (turbot) and *lüfer* (blue fish), a meaty fish best in autumn and winter. The following suggestions are on or around the routes in this book. For price guidelines: inexpensive signifies $16–25 for two, excluding wine; moderate, $25–50; and expensive $50 plus.

In Old Istanbul

Asitane
Kariye Hotel, Kariye Camii Sok. 18
Edirnekapı
Tel: (0212) 5348414
Ottoman cuisine in historic setting near the Kariye Hotel. Expensive.

Balıkçı Sabahattin
Cankurtaran, Sultanahmet
Tel: (0212) 4581824
Seafood favourite since 1927. Moderate.

Darüzziyafe
Şifahane Sok. 6
Süleymaniye Complex, Beyazıt
Tel: (0212) 5118414
Ottoman-style restaurant in old kitchens of 16th-century mosque complex, catering for large groups. No alcohol. Moderate.

Doy-Doy
Sifa Hamami Sok. 13
Tel: (0212) 5171588
Satisfying kebabs, pizza, *meze* and salads, with plenty of vegetarian options. No credit cards. Inexpensive.

Hamdi Et Lokantasi
Tahimis Cad., Kalçın Sok. No 17, Eminönü
Tel: (0212) 5280390/5125424
Good kebabs. Inexpensive.

Havuzlu Restaurant
Gani Çelebi Sok. PTT Yani 3, Kapalı Çarşı
Tel: (0212) 5273346
Best of the restaurants in the Covered Bazaar; kebabs and delicious *meze*. Inexpensive.

Konyalı
Topkapı Palace
Tel: (0212) 5139696
Known for its delicious lamb specialities and vegetable dishes. Lunch only. Moderate.

Olimpiyat 2 Minas Restaurant
Samsa Sok. 7, Kumkapı
Tel: (0212) 5172240
A long-established fish restaurant in the colourful Armenian quarter. One of about 50 fish restaurants in a tiny area. Take time to wander round and choose. Moderate.

Pandeli Restaurant
Mısır Çarsısı, Eminönü
Tel: (0212) 5225534
Serves excellent fish and meat dishes in a historic setting. Moderate.

Rami
Utangaç Sok. 6, Cankurtaran
Tel: (0212) 5176593
In an old Ottoman house with antique-decorated rooms on three floors and candlelit balcony overlooking Blue Mosque in summer. Delicious, traditional Turkish food.

Above: breakfast with a view

Open daily noon–3pm, 7–11pm. No credit cards. Expensive

Sarnıç Restaurant
Soğukçeşme Sok., Sultanahmet
Tel: (0212) 5124291
Turkish and Continental cuisine in a cavernous underground cistern. Expensive.

Seasons Restaurant
Four Seasons Hotel, Tevfikhane Sokak 1
Tel: (0212) 6388200
Prisoners in the Ottoman jail that is now the Four Seasons Hotel would have been blown away by some of the finest food in Istanbul. Fabulous views and European-Asian fusion cuisine. Open lunch and dinner. Expensive.

Türkistan Aşevi
Tavukhane Sokak 36, Sultanahmet
Tel: (0212) 6386525
Settle in for the day, writing postcards and people-watching on the terrace of this delightful café-restaurant overlooking the Hippodrome. The service is delightful, the eastern Anatolian food delicious. No alcohol. Open daily 7am–11pm. Moderate.

Zeyrekhane Restaurant
Sinanağa Mahallesi,
Ibadethane Arkası Sokak 10,
Zeyrek, Fatih
Tel: (0212) 5322778
A restored Ottoman house with terrace overlooking the Golden Horn, this is out of the way but worth the effort for views, traditional Ottoman cuisine and friendly service. Lighter lunches available. Booking advised. Open Tue–Sun 9am–10pm. Moderate.

On the Bosphorus

Ali Baba
Kireçburnu Caddesi 20, Sarıyer
Tel: (0212) 2620889
Serves memorable fish grills, stews, and *meze*. Open noon–midnight. Moderate.

Bekriya
Birinci Cad. 90, 2nd floor, Arnavutköy
Tel: (0212) 2570469
Fashionably Bohemian *meyhane*. Menu includes some Balkan specialities. Open 11am–1am. No credit cards. Moderate.

Huzur
Salacak Iskelesi 20, Üsküdar
Tel: (0216) 3333157
A long-established and relaxed fish restaurant with a terrific view (especially at sunset) across to the European side of the Bosphorus. Open noon–midnight. No credit cards. Moderate.

Iskele
Vapur Iskelesi yanı 10, Çengelköy
Tel: (0216) 3215506
Set in a garden with a fabulous view of the Bosphorus. Excellent fish and tasty *meze*. Expensive.

Kanaat
Selmanipak Cad. 25, Üsküdar
Tel: (0216) 3333791
A traditional *lokanta* that has been here since the 1930s, Kanaat offers cheap and cheerful Turkish food with superb desserts, a short walk from the Üsküdar landing. Open daily 6am–11pm. No credit cards. Inexpensive.

Kıyı
Kefeliköy Cad. 126, Tarabya
Tel: (0212) 2620002/2696920
Fashionable fish restaurant decorated with original works by famous Turkish painters artists. Open noon-midnight. Expensive.

Kordon
Kuleli Caddesi 51, Çengelk
Tel: (0216) 3210473
Part of the chic Sumahan on the Water hotel, the, this sleek shorefront terrace restaurant in a former raki distillery has a splendid ro-

Above: fish with red peppers

mantic setting, fresh seafood and Mediterranean cuisine. A café-bar serves light meals.

Körfez
Körfez Cad. 78, Kanlıca
Tel: (0216) 4134314/4134098
A chic fish restaurant with a romantic setting. A boat runs across the Bosphorus from Rumeli Fortress by appointment. Noon–3pm, 7pm–midnight. Closed Mon. Major cards except Prestige. Expensive.

Laledan
Çırağan Palace Hotel Kempinski, Beşiktaş
Tel: (0212) 2583377
High-quality international cuisine, in a fabulous setting on the shore of the Bosphorus. Terrace open in summer; live music, seafood specials Monday and Tuesday. Open daily 7am–11pm. Expensive. The hotel also has an excellent Turkish restaurant, Tuğra.

Vogue
Spor Cad. 92, BJK Plaza A Blok 13, Akaretler, Beşiktaş
Tel: (0212) 2272545
Superb view, chic decor, great sushi, fusion food and cocktails. Join the beautiful people. Open 10.30am–3pm, 7pm–midnight. Expensive.

Yeni Iskele
Iskele Sok. 17
Yeniköy
Tel: (0212) 2623549
Seafood specialities. Moderate.

In New Istanbul
Çatı Restaurant
Istiklâl Cad., Orhan Apaydın Sok. 20/7, Beyoğlu
Tel: (0212) 2510000
Moderate prices and good service. Specialises in grilled meats. Live Turkish pop music in the evenings.

Changa, Taksim
Siraselviler Cad. 87/1
Tel: (0212) 2491348
Watch the chefs through the glass floor at this *uber*-cool Pacific-fusion restaurant with a menu by London chef, Peter Gordon. It has a reputation as one of the best restaurants in Europe, so book. Closed Sun. Expensive.

Çiçek Pasaji & Nevezade Sokak
Istiklal Cad., Beyoğlu
These two small passageways, former markets, are crammed with *meyhanes*, rowdy with violinists and happy tourists. Go for the atmosphere and good, if unexciting, food.

Evim
Büyük Parmakkapı Sok. 32/2, Beyoğlu
Tel: (0212) 2934025
Superb Black Sea cooking as well as some imaginative international food. Cheap, cosy and popular with students. No credit cards.

Four Seasons
Istiklâl Cad. 509, Tünel
Tel: (0212) 2933941
Elegant Turkish and European cuisine. Open noon–3pm and 6pm–midnight. Expensive, but superb value fixed-price lunch menu.

Galata House
Galata Kulesi Sok. 61, Galata
Tel: (0212) 2451861
Once the British prison, the food is Georgian, Russian and Tartar and there is sometimes live piano. Great fun. Tue–Sun noon–midnight.

Galata Tower Restaurant
Galata Kulesi, Karaköy
Tel: (0212) 2938180
Situated in the 14th-century Genoese Tower with a great view of Istanbul. Floor show with belly dancing. Bookings are necessary. Expensive.

Left: Galata Tower

Hacı Abdullah
Sakızağa Cad. 17, Beyoğlu
Tel: (0212) 2938561
A famous and very old traditional *lokanta*, serving wonderful home cooking. No alcohol. Open 11.30am–10pm. Inexpensive.

Hacı Baba
Istiklâl Cad., Meşelik Sok. 49, Taksim
Tel: (0212) 2441886
Classic Turkish restaurant serving grills and baked lamb. A wonderful view from the terrace to the gardens of a Greek church below. Booking advised in summer. Moderate.

Hünal's Brasserie
Araketler Sıraevleri
Spor Cad. 1, Beşiktaş
Tel: (0212) 2593030
In a restored mansion, this trendy restaurant offers international cuisine and an outdoor summer terrace. The North Shield English Pub is below the restaurant. Moderate.

Kaktüs
Imam Adnan Sok. (off Istiklal), Beyoğlu
Tel: (0212) 292 5979
Tiny, Parisian-style bistro with arty clientèle. Bar, espressos, pasta. Open Mon–Sat 9am–2am, Sun 11am–2am.

Kallavi 20
Istiklâl Cad., Kallavi Sok. 20, Beyoğlu
Tel: (0212) 2511010
Excellent set meal, accompanied by Turkish music. Closed Sun. No cards. Moderate.

KV Café
Tünel Geçidi 10, Tünel
Tel: (0212) 2514338
Enchanting café opposite the top station of the Tünel. Coffee, tea and cake, light meals and drinks. Romantic garden and simple brick, candlelit rooms. Open daily 8am–1.30am.

Machka Russian Restaurant
Abdi Ipekçi Cad. 48, Maçka
Tel: (0212) 2405729
Expensive Russian cuisine in chic environment. Many varieties of vodka. Closed Sun.

Refik's
Sofyalı Sok. 10–12, Tünel

Tel: (0212) 2432834
Funky favourite in the Asmalımescıt, specialising in Black Sea dishes. The good-natured owner is an institution, but service can be slow, bills muddled. Open noon–midnight, closed Sun. No credit cards. Inexpensive.

Refika
Mesrutiyet Sok. 149, Beyoğlu
Tel: (0212) 2455652
New York minimalist decor with American food such as chicken pot pie. Sunday brunch includes pancakes and eggs Benedict. Pricey, but seriously stylish. Open 10am–7pm, closed Mon. No alcohol.

Rejans
Emir Nevruz Sok. 17, Galatasaray-Beyoğlu
Tel: (0212) 2441610
Founded in the 1920s by Russian refugees and once the city's most stylish restaurant. Today it serves *piroshki*, *borscht*, stewed duck, etc. Reservations are recommended. Noon–3pm, 7–11pm, closed Sun. Moderate.

Sunset Grill Bar
Ahmet Adnan Saygun Cad., Kireçhane Sok., Ulus Park
Tel: (0212) 2870357
This Californian-style restaurant offers and exquisite view of the Bosphorus. Mainly grills. Fashionable; 7pm–midnight. All major cards. Expensive.

Yakup 2
Asmalımescıt Sok. 35/37, Tünel
Tel: (0212) 2492925
A genuine Turkish tavern. Casual and noisy, but a lot of fun. Open noon–2am. Moderate.

Near the Airport

Beyti Restaurant
Orman Sok. 8, Florya
Tel: (0212) 6632992
One of the best meat restaurants. Huge, with a dozen rooms and a terrace. Moderate.

Kasibeyaz
Çatal Sok. 10
Tel: (0212) 6332890
Specialising in spicy, eastern Turkish cuisine, it's popular with locals at weekends when you'll need to book. Moderate.

NIGHTLIFE

On a sultry summer's night, there's no escaping the crowds. The well-heeled head for the cool seaside fish restaurants and nightclubs. Café society spills out onto the streets at Ortaköy, Moda and Kadife Sokak.

Streets can be impassable in Beyoğlu, where the young head for the cinemas, *meyhanes* (taverns), or rave and heavy-metal bars that pulse around Taksim Square. Close to Istiklâl are French-style bistros, popular among the intelligentsia, along with student dives offering cheap lager. The legal drinking age is 18 and it is necessary to carry ID.

For the young, rave and techno clubs abound, but cover charges are high. Jazz cafés catering to an older crowd also have high cover charges. Among the best are the Gramafon (tel: (0212) 2930786) next to the Tünel stop on Istiklal; or Babylon in Asmalımescit (tel: (0212) 2927368), which models itself on New York's Knitting Factory, offering cutting-edge jazz with significant Turkish input. The intimate Nardiz Jazz Club (Kuledibi Sok 14, Galata, tel: (0212) 2446327) has nightly jazz of every style and nationality; and the waterfront Istanbul Jazz Café (Cirağan Caddesi 48, Ortaköy, tel: (0212) 3275050) is a major venue in the Istanbul Jazz Festival.

Gay nightlife is easily found, but venues vary from friendly to the decidedly rough, so travellers should be cautious. Bar Bahçe, Siraselviler Caddesi, Soganci Sokak 7/1, Cihangir; TT's, Sehit Muhtar Caddesi, Ilkyaz Apt 2/2, Taksim; and the Queen Bar, Istiklal Caddesi Zambak Sok. 23, Taksim are safe, friendly and good starting points.

There are numerous traditional Kurdish/Anatolian cafés such as the Historical Pano Wine House (Tarihi Pano Çaraphanesi Balik Pazar, Meşrutiyet Cad., tel: (0212) 2926664), which dates from 1898. You have to get in early, even for standing room. Ora, above Kaktüs on Imam Adnan Sok, is friendly and is also cheap.

For a quietly satisfying night glorying in Istanbul, head to one of the many rooftop bars or restaurants. To see and be seen, have a cocktail at 360 (Iştikal Caddesi 311; (0212) 2511042/3); Leb-i-Derya (Kumbaraci Yokusu 115/7, Tünel; tel: (0212) 293 4989); or Mikla (the Marmara Pera Hotel, 17/F Marmara Pera, Mesrutiyet Caddesi, Beyoğlu; tel: (0212) 2935656).

Belly-dancing is primarily a tourist show, often put on in the main hotels and at the restaurant-cum-nightclub on top of the Galata Tower, though it can be a family affair in seaside restaurants. Either way, spectators are expected to tip the dancer. Nightlife in Sultanahmet tends to be quiet, since this is primarily a religious neighbourhood. But there are worse ways of spending an evening than relaxing in a Sultanahmet tea garden, perhaps smoking a water-pipe and watching old men play the Turkish dice game, *tavla*.

Above: musicians take a well-earned break

CALENDAR OF EVENTS

Specific dates for some of the following events vary from year to year. Check with the tourist office.

March–April

Istanbul International Film Festival
Scores of new foreign and Turkish films compete for top prizes. A good opportunity for film aficionados to view a wide spectrum of international movies at different cinemas throughout the city, as well as Turkish films with English subtitles. Renowned film-makers and actors are invited as guests or as jury members. Awards include the Golden Tulip, the grand prize of the festival, the Special Prize of the Jury, awarded to an individual, and the Life Achievement Award.

May–June

Istanbul International Theatre Festival
Lasting for about a month, this festival allows theatre companies from around the world to perform new plays before Turkish and international audiences. Each play is performed in the original language, with digital subtitles in Turkish.

The Conquest of Istanbul
On 29 May the anniversary of the Turkish conquest of Istanbul in 1453 is celebrated, re-enacting battles between Janissaries and Byzantines along the Byzantine walls. Parades are held featuring the Mehter (Ottoman Marching Band).

Mid-June – end of July

Istanbul International Music Festival
This music festival showcases both orchestral and chamber music, along with recitals, opera, ballet, modern dance and Turkish classical music. Some opera and recitals take place in the Byzantine church Aya Irini, with plans afoot to utilise Beylerbeyı Palace. Famous orchestras such as the New York Philharmonic and the Berlin Symphony are featured, with ticket prices considerably lower than those charged in the rest of Europe.

Istanbul International Jazz Festival
Everything from classical jazz to the latest world/jazz fusion acts at numerous venues.

September–October (2007)

Istanbul International Biennial
One of the top four biennials worldwide, covering film, theatre, music and visual arts with hundreds of international artists.

CULTURAL AND PERFORMANCE VENUES

Aksanat
14-19 Istiklal Caddesi, Beyoğlu
Tel: (0212) 252 35000/1
An imaginative arts complex with theatre, film, music and exhibition space offering a wide variety of innovative work.

Atatürk Cultural Centre (AKM)
Taksim Square
Tel: (0212) 2515600/2433261
Venue shared by the State Opera, Ballet, Symphony Orchestra and Theatre Company.

Biletix
Tel: (0216) 5569800, www.biletix.com
The main ticket agency, with sales for all major events online, by phone or at one of numerous sales desks, eg the Ada Bookshop, Istiklâl Caddesi; Vakkorama, Etiler; Galleria Shopping Centre; and Kadıköy Ferry Pier.

Cemal Reşit Rey Concert Hall
Harbiye
Tel: (0212) 2329830
Large hall with varied programmes.

Istanbul Foundation for Culture and Arts
Istiklâl Cad., 146 Luvr Apt, Beyoğlu
Tel: (0212) 3340700
Responsible for all the Istanbul International Art festivals and Biennial.

Pamukbank Photograph Gallery
Teşvikiye Cad. 105/3
Tel: (0212) 2366790
Prestigious photographic exhibitions.

Turkish Cultural Dance Theatre
Fırat Culture Centre, Divanyolu Cad.
Çemberlitaş
Tel: (0212) 5178692
Regional Turkish dance on Mon, Wed and Sat night, including whirling dervishes.

Practical
Information

TRAVEL ESSENTIALS

Arriving by air

Most scheduled services use Atatürk International, 24km (15 miles) west of Istanbul city centre, on the European shore. From here, there are taxis (2 hrs at rush hour), hotel shuttle buses, Havaş shuttle buses every 30 mins to Akmerkez (Etiler, 45 mins) and Taksim (40 mins) and the metro that runs to Aksaray and is due to connect to Taksim in 2007. It connects with the tram at Zeytinburnu, if you want Sultanahmet and the Bosphorus shore.

Low-cost carriers arrive at Sabiha Gökçen, on the Asian side, 50km (30 miles) from Taksim. Shuttle buses to and from Bostancı connevt with ferries for the European side. Otherwise, the only transport is by taxi.

Visas

All visitors need a passport valid for at least six months. Nationals of Denmark, Finland, France, Germany, Greece, Israel, Japan, New Zealand, Sweden and Switzerland are among those who do not need a visa. Nationals of Australia, Austria, Belgium, Canada, Holland, Ireland, Italy, Portugal, Spain, the UK and USA need a visa, which is payable in cash (US$, UK£ or euros) at the booth before immigration. The price varies hugely from one country to the next. Photos are not needed. If in doubt, check the Turkish Ministry of Foreign Affairs website, www.mfa.gov.tr.

Climate

Summers are warm in Istanbul and winters are mild and damp with plenty of rainfall and the occasional short-lived blizzard. The best time to visit is May to June and September to October, as it can get uncomfortably hot and humid in July and August, forcing inhabitants to beaches along the Black Sea and Sea of Marmara to cool off. Average afternoon temperatures are as follows: January: 8°C (46°F), April: 16°C (61°F) July: 28°C (82°F), October: 20°C (68°F).

Left: tram on Istiklâl Caddesi
Right: local bus

What to wear

Take light, cotton clothing for the heat of summer and warm, waterproof clothing from November to March. While acceptable in resorts, skimpy clothing is not appropriate in the city.

Electricity

Electricity is 220-volt, 50-cycle. European plugs with two-round-prongs usually work.

Time

Turkish Standard Time is two hours ahead of Greenwich Mean Time and seven hours ahead of Eastern Standard Time. It advances by one hour (GMT+3) from Apr–Oct.

Business Hours

Government offices are open from 8.30am–noon and 1.30–5pm.

Public Holidays

January 1: New Year's Day
April 23: National Sovereignty and Children's Day
May 19: Youth and Sports Holiday and Atatürk's Commemoration.
August 30: Victory Day
October 29: Republic Day
In addition, there are two Muslim holidays for which dates vary: *Seker Bayramı* (Sweet Holiday), which follows Ramadan; and *Kurban Bayramı* (Feast of the Sacrifice).

GETTING AROUND

Metro and Tram

Rapid construction continues on the tram and metro systems providing cheap, fast, air-conditioned transport through the old city, to the airport, across the Golden Horn and along the European shore of the Bosphorus as far as Dolmabahce. The Tunnel leads up to Istiklal Caddesi from the Golden Horn and a funicular runs from Kabataş ferry port up to Taksim Square. Between the two, an antique tram runs along Istiklal. A second nostalgic tram runs between Kadıköy and Moda on the Asian shore. Tunnels under construction will carry the metro under the Golden Horn, to link up with the section from Taksim to Levent, and under the Bosphorus to link in Usküdar.

Ferries

The main city ferry ports include Eminönü, beside the Galata Bridge, Karaköy and Kabataş, Uskudar, Haydarpaşa and Kadıköy on the Asian side. The Bosphorus ferry doubles as a sightseeing trip. Most are run by Turkish Maritime Lines (www.tdi.com.tr) and Istanbul Fast Ferry (www.ido.com.tr). Timetables are available from the docks.

Istanbul Fast Ferries (tel: 444 4436; www.ido.com.tr) operates several routes across the Sea of Marmara and a regular Black Sea ferry to Odessa is run by UKR Ferry Shipping Company (www.ukrferry.com).

Tickets

All city metro, tram, bus, and ferry services work on 2YTL tokens (1 per journey) or an pre-paid Akbil ticket, a reusable plastic token that offers a small discount per journey. A blue (*mavi*) Akbil operates as a 1-day, 1-week, 15-day or 31-day travel card. Get all tickets from kiosks near the stations. For more information on all transport, go to www.iett.gov.tr.

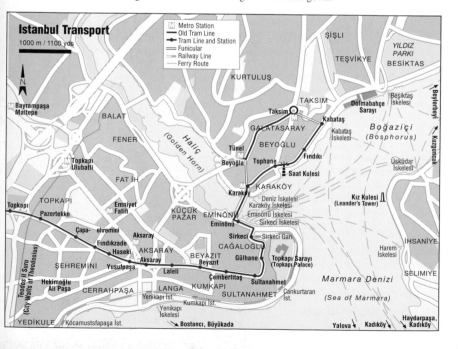

Taxis

Ubiquitous taxis are yellow and show a light if free, either at ranks in the street. Few drivers speak more than a few words of English, and you can't rely on them knowing their way around, so have your destination written down, preferably marked on a map. Most drivers are honest, but you may run into trouble in touristy areas such as the Grand Bazaar, where you will need to check the meter is switched on – and on the correct rate (one red light on the meter for day rate and two for evening) or fix the fare before you get in. Ask a local what the fare should be and haggle hard, as they may try to charge over the odds, put the meter on then drive in circles or use sleight of hand to confuse you with unfamiliar currency. The bridge toll over the Bosphorus will be added. There are few radio-controlled networks, but hotels, restaurants and shops will always be happy to find a cab for you. If you are looking at taking a lot of cabs, it may well be worth hiring a car and driver by the day.

Trains

Sirkeci Station, Eminönü (tel: (0212) 527 0050), handles all international traffic and trains from European Thrace and Marmara. Trains from Anatolian Turkey use Haydarpaşa Station (tel: (0216) 3488020) on the Asian shore. Both have suburban services. Book at the stations or via travel agents. For information visit www.tcdd.gov.tr.

Buses

The main long-distance transport is by coach with services coming in to Esenler Bus Terminal (Oto Gar), Bayrampaşa (tel: (0212) 658 0505/1010), 10km (6 miles) northwest of the centre on the European side and the Harem Bus Terminal next to Haydarpaşa on the Asian side. Reputable companies include Kamil Koç (www.kamkoc.com.tr), Ulusoy (www.ulusoy.com.tr), Pamukkale (www.pamukkaleturizm.com.tr) and Varan (www.varan.com.tr). Bookings can be made in the UK via Eurolines (www.eurolines.co.uk; tel: 0870 580 8080).

Car

Having a car is a major disadvantage in the city, with massive traffic jams, huge difficulties in parking and difficult driving conditions. If wanting to head out of town or to visit a number of more scattered sights, consider hiring a car with a driver by the day. At the time of writing, the price was running at about YTL200 per day, including fuel, parking, bridge tolls and the driver. This can be arranged via any travel agent or hotel reception desk. All the main car hire firms have offices at the airports and in Istanbul.

Car Hire

Avis *www.avis.com.*
Budget *www.budget.com.*
Europcar *www.europcar.com.*
Hertz *www.hertz.com.*
Reliable local firms include **Thrifty-Decar** tel: (0212) 4654525, www.decar.com.tr and **Sixt Rent a Car** tel: (0212) 6632587/8, www.sixt.com.tr.

TOURIST INFORMATION

UK: *4th Floor, 29-30 St. James's Street, London, SW1A 1HB Tel: 020 7839 7778, www.gototurkey.co.uk*
USA: *821 United Nations Plaza, New York NY 10017*
Tel: (1-212) 687-2194 9596
www.tourismturkey.org
Istanbul: *Hilton Hotel Lobby*
Tel: (0212) 2330592
Ataturk International Airport
Tel: (0212) 6630793 Visit the airport office on arrival to pick up maps and brochures. *Divanyolu Cad. Otobus Durağı Arkası 3, Sultanahmet*
Tel: (0212) 5181802

Left: traffic jams are a problem
Right: Haydarpasa Station

MONEY MATTERS

In 2005, six noughts were knocked off the currency, taking the lira from 2,500,000 to £1 to 2.5 to £1. The slide in value continues, but more slowly. Yeni (New) Turkish lira (YTL) come in YTL 1, 5, 10, 20, 50 and 100 notes and YTL1 coins. YTL1 is split into 100 kuruş (1, 5, 10, 20 kuruş coins). You may bring unlimited foreign currency and up to US$5,000 worth of YTL into Turkey.

Most banks cash travellers' cheques and foreign currency, but *döviz* (change) offices are everywhere and give better rates. Some remain open at weekends. Banks are open Mon–Fri 8.30am–noon and 1.30–5pm; some main branches open Sat am and there are 24-hour banks at the airport. ATMs are plentiful and most sales-people are happy to deal in US$, euros or sterling. Few outlets, including hotels, accepts travellers' cheques.

Tipping

A service charge of 10 percent is usually included in restaurant bills. Waiters expect an additional 5 percent; barmen expect to be tipped. In hotels, tips for services should be given on the spot. Do not tip taxi drivers.

MEDIA

Turkey's one daily English-language newspaper, the *Turkish Daily News*, is published in Ankara. Most major foreign publications are available. English-language magazines, offering information and listings, available from newsagents and hotels, include *The Guide* (www.theguideistanbul.com), *Time Out, Istanbul Forever* and *Cornucopia* (www.cornucopia.net). Foreign-language booksops include:

Homer Kitapevi
Yeniçarşi Cad. 28A, Beyoğlu
Tel: (0212) 2495902
Librairie de Pera
Galip Dede Cad. 22, Tünel
Tel: (0212) 2523078
www.librairiedepera.com.tr
Natural Foreign Book Exchange
Akbıyık Cad, Sultanahmet
Tel: (0212) 5170383

COMMUNICATIONS

Telephone

Phone calls can be made from the Post Office (PTT) using tokens *(jeton)*. A small *jeton* is for local calls, a large *jeton* is for international calls. You can also use a phone card for lengthy calls. Most public phones now use phone cards. Phone shops marked 'Kontur Telefon' allow you to make calls and pay at the end. European-standard GSM mobile phones are common. When calling the Asian side of Istanbul from the European side dial (0216) first and then the number. If you call the European side from the Asian side, dial (0212) followed by the number.

International Calls

First dial the international access code 00, then the country code: Australia (61); France (33); Germany (49); Netherlands (31); Spain (34); UK (44); US and Canada (1). If using a US credit phone card, dial the company's access number which you should ascertain before leaving home. You can send telex, fax messages and telegrams from the PTT.

Mail Services

The Turkish postal service is usually reliable. There is a fixed charge for letters abroad; postcards are a little cheaper. The main post offices remain open long hours: Mon–Sat 8am–midnight, Sun 9am–7pm.

HEALTH/EMERGENCIES

Visitors in need of emergency medical treatment should visit one of the foreign hospitals *(hastane)*. Many Turkish doctors *(doktor)* have been trained abroad and speak other languages. For minor injuries go to a dispensary *(dispanser)* or even a drugstore *(eczane)*. Antibiotics can be obtained at drugstores without a prescription.

Water

Tap water in Istanbul has a rather disagreeable taste because it is so heavily chlorinated. This makes it safe to drink but travellers anywhere in Turkey are generally advised to drink bottled water as far as possible. This is sold everywhere and is inexpensive.

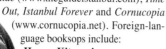

Left: traditional dress

Hospitals

The main foreign hospitals are:

Amiral Bristol Amerikan Hastanesi (American Hospital)
Güzelbahçe Sok., Nişantaşı
Tel: (0212) 3112000

Florence Nightingale Hospital
Abide Hürriyet Cad. 290, Şişli
Tel: (0212) 2244950

International Hospital
Istanbul Cad. 82, Yeşilyurt
Tel: (0212) 6633000

Medline *(tel: 4441212 – no area code; www.medline.com.tr)* offers a full private medical emergency service, with road and air ambulances and motorbike paramedics. **General Ambulance** *(tel: (0212) 5412917/ 19; mobile. (0532) 3123129)* also has private ambulances and a helicopter service.

SECURITY AND CRIME

Violent crime is rare. Single women often attract attention and should use common sense. Otherwise, you can walk down any street in Istanbul late at night without fear. Beware of pickpockets on crowded streets and in tourist areas such as Istiklâl and near the Hilton. For police *(polis)* assistance, go to the *karakol* (police station). Dial 155 in emergencies. If you experience harassment by touts, bill fiddling or theft, contact the Tourism Police (0212-5274503) near Yerebatan Saray in Sultanahmet. Possession of narcotics, including hashish, is punishable by life imprisonment. The vast majority of Turks are pro-Western and moderate in their beliefs. There have been bombs, but the threat of terrorist attack is no greater than in London or New York.

ACCOMMODATION

Old Istanbul

US$250/£150 and above

The Four Seasons
Tevkifhane Sok. 1, Sultanahmet
Tel: (0212) 6388200
Fax: (0212) 6388210
www.fourseasons.com
A restored neo-classical Ottoman prison is now one of the city's most luxurious and

prestigious hotels. Wonderful views of Aya Sofya and Blue Mosque, top-notch service, splendid décor, Ottoman antiques and all mod cons. Small and popular, so be sure to book well ahead.

US$120–250/£70–150

Ayasofya Konaklari
Soğukçeşme Sok, Sultanahmet
Tel: (0212) 5133660
Fax: (0212) 5133669
www.ayasofyakonaklari.com
A 19th-century cobbled lane of wooden houses along the outer wall of the Topkapi Palace has been restored to make nine delightful guesthouses. Rooms are renovated in a tasteful blend of contemporary and Ottoman styles. There is a magnificent view of Aya Sofya from the more expensive rooms.

Kariye Hotel
Kariye Camii Sok. 18, Edirnekapı
Tel: (0212) 5348414
Fax: (0212) 5216631
www.kariyeotel.com
This elegant hotel with 22 rooms, 5 suites and a garden pavilion, in a restored Ottoman mansion, is next to one of Istanbul's most exceptionally preserved churches. A superb restaurant specialises in historic Ottoman dishes and traditional court music.

Mavi Ev (Blue House)
Dalbastı Sok 14, Sultanahmet
Tel: (0212) 6389010

Above: view of Galata Bridge from the Galata Tower

www.armadahotel.com.tr
A reconstruction of a terrace of houses originally built for a 16th-century Ottoman
admiral. Offers views of Aya Sofya and the
Blue Mosque, and has two good restaurants
and a bar.

Hotel Ayasofya
Küçükayasofya Mah,
Demirci Reşit Sok. 28, Sultanahmet
Tel: (0212) 5169446
Fax: (0212) 5180700
www.ayasofyahotel.com
In a 19th-century house, this 21-room hotel has been rebuilt and restored in Ottoman
style. Benefits from a good location in the
Old City close to the Blue Mosque and Topkapı Palace.

www.bluehouse.com.tr
This truly charming restored Ottoman house
hotel just behind the Blue Mosque is a real
home-from-home, with friendly staff, a great
location, simply but comfortably furnished
rooms, a rooftop restaurant with spectacular
views and free wi-fi and internet.

Hotel Celal Sultan
Salkımsöğüt Sok. 16, Yerebatan Cad.,
Sultanahmet
Tel: (0212) 5209323/24
Fax: (0212) 5229742
www.celalsultan.com
This classically restored, cosy townhouse
has a great view from the roof terrace of Aya
Sofya, the Blue Mosque and the Sea of
Marmara. There are 2 suites and 55 rooms,
some with balconies, and all double glazed
and with cable TV.

Yeşil Ev
Kabasakal Cad. 5, Sultanahmet
Tel: (0212) 5176785
Fax: (0212) 5176780
www.istanbulyesilev.com/en
A restored wooden mansion, previously the
home of an Ottoman paşa, in an excellent
location between Aya Sofya and the Blue
Mosque. The 18 small rooms and 1 suite are
simply appointed but nicely decorated in Ottoman style. There is an attractive, walled
rear garden with conservatory and good
restaurant. Book well in advance.

Empress Zöe
Akbüyük Cad., Adliye Sok. 10
Tel: (0212) 5184360
Fax: (0212) 5185699
www.emzoe.com
Situated near the Topkapı Palace, this American-owned hotel has 22 individually decorated, air-conditioned rooms and suites. There
are Byzantine wall paintings, antiques, and
the ruins of a 15th-century Turkish bath in the
garden. The terrace bar has great views.

Under US$120/£70
Ambassador Hotel
Divanyolu Ticarethane Sokak 19,
Sultanahmet
Tel: (0212) 5120002
Fax (0212) 5120005
www.istanbulambassadorhotel.com
Close to the Blue Mosque with views over
the Sea of Marmara. Reasonably comfortable, with grill restaurant and bar. Breakfast is served in the top-floor terrace.

Hotel Fehmi Bey
Üçler Sok. 15, Sultanahmet
Tel: (0212) 6389083/85
Fax: (0212) 5181264
www.fehmibey.com
Housed in a restored townhouse just by the
Hippodrome, this family-run hotel offers
34 small, comfortable rooms, a sauna and
a spectacular sea view from its roof terrace.

Armada Hotel
Ahırkapı Sokak 24, Sultanahmet
Tel: (0212) 4554455
Fax: (0212) 4554499

Above: public telephone

Hotel Hippodrome

Mimar Mehmet Aga Cad. 38
Sultanahmet
Tel: (0212) 5176889
Fax: (0212) 6160268
Small, comfortable and hospitable hotel set in an Ottoman house between Aya Sofya and the Blue Mosque, of which there are stunning views from the terrace. Rooms have en suite facilities and are well-equipped.

Ibrahim Paşa

Terzihane Sok. 5, Adliye Yani,
Sultanahmet
Tel: (0212) 5180394
Fax: (0212) 5184457
www.ibrahimpasha.com
Small, stylish and understated, this French-owned hotel, with a Parisian ambience, is set in a renovated 19th-century Ottoman townhouse next to the Hippodrome. The 19 rooms are smallish and simply furnished but friendly staff and excellent breakfasts compensate. Spectacular view of the Blue Mosque and Sea of Marmara from the roof terrace.

Hotel Kybele

Yerebatan Cad. 35
Sultanahmet
Tel: (0212) 5117766/67
Fax: (0212) 5134393
www.kybelehotel.com
A treasure house of Ottoman antiques and kilims, with a lobby lit by 1,000 antique lamps. There are 16 comfortable, air-conditioned rooms with marble bathrooms, a restaurant and a delightful courtyard. English, Japanese and other languages are spoken by the helpful staff.

New Istanbul
US$225/£150 and above
Ceylan Inter-Continental Hotel

Asker Ocaği Cad. 1, Taksim
Tel: (0212) 3684444
Fax: (0212) 3684499
www.ichotelsgroup.com
This luxurious hotel commands superb views of the Bosphorus and city skylines. Restaurants include Turkish, French and Californian cuisine and there are bars and de luxe banqueting and convention facilities, sports facilities and shops.

Çırağan Palace Hotel Kempinski

Çırağan Cad., Beşiktaş
Tel: (0212) 3264646
Fax: (0212) 2596687
www.ciraganpalace.com
A superb (expensive) hotel in a restored Ottoman palace on the European banks of the Bosphorus, near the city centre. Excellent Ottoman and Italian restaurants. Offers a range of rooms and suites, some in the original palace. Beautiful outdoor pool and outdoor jazz club.

Conrad Hotel

Barbaros Bulvarı, Yıldız Cad., Beşiktaş
Tel: (0212) 2273000
Fax: (0212) 2596667
www.conradhotels.com
Conveniently located, this well-equipped modern hotel also has wonderful views of the Bosphorus and Yıldız Imperial Gardens. Good Italian and Turkish restaurants and French patisserie, plud live jazz in the bar, a health club with indoor and outdoor pools, and a 24-hour business centre.

Hilton Istanbul

Cumhuriyet Cad., Harbiye
Tel: (0212) 3156000
Fax: (0212) 2404165
www.hilton.com
Set away from the traffic in extensive and tranquil grounds, this 1950s hotel is still one of the best in Istanbul, renowned for its good service. It has 483 good-size rooms and 15 suites and has been fully renovated and lavishly decorated in recent years. There are seven bars and restaurants, and facilities include a health club and spa, an outdoor pool, and special service for business travellers.

Right: Ayasofya Konaklari

Hyatt Regency Istanbul
Taşkişla Cad., Taksim
Tel: (0212) 3681234
Fax: (0212) 3681000
www.istanbul.hyatt.com
Decorated in a mix of modern and Ottoman styles. Business travellers well catered for.

The Marmara Istanbul
Taksim Meydani, 80090, Taksim
Tel: (0212) 2514696
Fax: (0212) 2440509

www.themarmara.com
New Istanbul's best known, business and conference hotel. The Panorama restaurant offers superb views, and there is the popular Café Marmara on the ground floor.

Swissôtel The Bosphorus
Bayıldım Cad. 2, Maçka
Tel: (0212) 3261100
Fax: (0212) 3261122
www.swissotel.com
Located directly behind the Dolmabahçe Palace, this massive hotel has a huge, lavish lobby but fairly plain rooms. The service is excellent and there are superb views of the Topkapi Palace and beyond.

US$120–225/£80–150
Anemon Galata
Büyükhendek Cad. 11, Kuledibi Beyoğlu
Tel: (0212) 2932343
Fax: (0212) 2922340
www.anemonhotels.com
Restored old house with 23 rooms and 7 suites, in a perfect position right beside the

INSIGHT Pocket Guides

The travel guides that replace a tour guide - now better than ever with more listings and a fresh new design

Galata Tower. The rooftop bar and restaurant have a fabulous view over the Bosphorus.

Divan Hotel
Cumhuriyet Cad. 2, Elmadağ
Tel: (0212) 3155500
Fax: (0212) 3155515
www.divanhotel.com.tr
Friendly and efficient, with 180 spacious, comfortable rooms. Good restaurant.

Pera Palas Hotel
Meşrutiyet Cad. 98/100, Tepebaşı
Tel: (0212) 2514560
Fax: (0212) 2514088
www.perapalas.com
The historic Orient Express hotel has hosted Kemal Atatürk, Agatha Christie and Mata Hari. The splendid lobby has a marble staircase and elaborate lift; the 139 rooms and six suites are slightly faded but atmospheric.

Richmond Hotel
Istiklâl Cad. 445, Beyoğlu
Tel: (0212) 2525460
Fax: (0212) 2529707
www.richmondhotels.com.tr
Recently renovated 19th-century building in the heart of Beyoğlu, 10 minutes' walk to the Old City. Set on a precinct which is free of traffic except for the retro trams trundling by.

Under US$120/£80
Büyük Londra Hotel
Meşrutiyet Cad. 117, Tepebaşı, Beyoğlu
Tel. (0212) 2450670
Fax: (0212) 245 0671
www.londrahotel.net
By the Golden Horn; the Ottoman-style furnishings are faded originals. There is an atmospheric lobby full of Italian chandeliers, and an extremely cheap bar. Rock bottom rates (with a substantial breakfast). Some of the 54 rooms have sea-views. Book early.

Vardar Palace Hotel
Şiraselyiler Cad. 54–56, Taksim
Tel: (0212) 2522888
Fax: (0212) 2521527
www.vardarhotel.com.tr
Great central location with friendly service. Built in 1901 in the Levantine-Selçuk style, and carefully restored. Forty rooms.

Villa Zurich
Akarsu Yokuşu Cad. 44–6, Cihangir
Tel: (0212) 2930604
Fax: (0212) 2490232
www.hotelvillazurich.com
Comfortable hotel with 43 rooms, an excellent fish restaurant and a roof terrace. Within walking distance of Taksim Square.

Apart-Hotels (Apartments)
Galata Residence Hotel
Bankalar Cad., Hacı Ali Sok., Galata
Tel: (0212) 2924841
Fax: (0212) 2442323
www.galataresidence.com
This 19th-century mansion near the Galata Tower has been elegantly restored; 7 one-bedroom and 15 two-bedroom apartments, with fully equipped kitchens and bathrooms.

Near the Airport
US$120/£80 and above
Çinar Hotel
Sevketiye Mah, Fener Mevkii, Yeşilköy
Tel: (0212) 6632900
Fax: (0212) 6632921
In a quiet spot on the shores of the Sea of Marmara. There are 213 rooms and 8 suites. Three restaurants, indoor and outdoor pools, a fitness centre and a cinema.

Crowne Plaza Istanbul
Sahil Yolu, 34710 Ataköy
Tel: (0212) 5608100
Fax: (0212) 5608158
www.ichotelsgroup.com
In several acres of gardens near the airport, overlooking the Sea of Marmara, this hotel has a regular shuttle service to the historic sites. Sports facilities include a health club, pools, tennis courts and a jogging track.

Over the Bosphorus
US$150/£100 and above
Sumahan Hotel
Kuleli Caddesi 51, Çengelköy, Asian Side
Tel: (0216) 422 80 00
www.sumahan.com
A super-cool little boutique hotel in a converted raki distillery on the Bosphorus. Each of the 18 rooms and suites is individually decorated in contemporary style, all have sea views and some have their own *hamams*.

Left: the Conrad Hotel

practical information

ACKNOWLEDGEMENTS

Photography	Phil Wood and Marcus Wilson-Smith
Additional Photography	
35B	AKG London
53	Steve Bly
28	Nevzat Çakır
71	Metin Demirsar
60, 62	Mehmet Erdur
45T	Nermi Erdur
16, 23B, 24, 42, 48, 49, 50, 61B, 64, 72	Ara Güler
40, 41, 43, 46, 52, 57T, 61T, 75T, 75B, 79,	
80, 83, 88	Şemsi Güner
76	Keribar/FOG
8/9	Kısmet/FOG
56	Enis Özbank
2/3	Şakir/FOG
39	TKB
Front Cover	Photodisc Red/Getty Images
Cartography	Maria Donnelly
Cover Design	Klaus Geisler

© APA Publications GmbH & Co. Verlag KG Singapore Branch, Singapore

INDEX